BECOMING GOD'S DAUGHTER
From a Prodigal To a Princess

A Memoir Breathed by the Holy Spirit
Written by P.T. Grimes

Cover Design: Luminous Publishing
Cover Photo: Pharris Photos & Films PharrisPhotos.com

Publishing in the United States of America Publisher:
Luminous Publishing www.luminouspublishing.com
For bulk orders or other inquiries, email:
info@luminouspublishing.com

This book is dedicated to my heavenly Father, who sees me, accepts me, and loves me unconditionally.

To all the daughters and (sons) of God who are still trying to find their TRUE identity…

The Father planted you as His seed, the Holy Spirit waters you, and the Son helps you grow!

- P.T. Grimes

TABLE OF CONTENTS

CHAPTER 1

❧

Introduction

Panic, Pandemic, Shelter in Place

It is March 21, 2020, and I am home in South Florida, processing the events and life situations that brought me here. The coronavirus pandemic has spread all over the world. Adults and children alike are quarantined in their homes. Schools have closed. Thousands have lost their jobs and lives. For many, life has made a 360-degree turn. Socializing, hugging, shaking hands, and making social contact are avoided. Social distancing is a must. When going out, people wear masks, gloves, and purchase hand sanitizer as if it were water. This airborne disease is very contagious and deadly.

The world is in a place of the unknown. People are either out of work or working from home. Children are learning virtually. Working remotely has become the new norm across the globe. As an educator, my world has been interrupted. I am trying to find a new effective approach in educating my students and reassuring parents that I am here for them.

In my own world, there rests the cares and worries of the future. My family's health and safety, friends, church family, bills, financial obligations, and yes, even obtaining tissue are at the forefront of my thoughts. But then there is something, or should I say "someone" who is at the core of these thoughts. It begs me to ask this one question that increased my anxiety about the future:

God, what are You up to?

The Farmer sows the Word. Some people are like seed along the path, where the Word is sown. As soon as they hear it, Satan comes and takes away the Word that was sown in them. Others, like the seed sown on rocky places, hear the Word and at once receive it with joy. But since they have no root, they last only a short time. When trouble or persecution comes because of the Word, they quickly fall away. Still others, like seed sown among thorns, hear the Word; but the worries of this life, the deceitfulness of wealth and the desires for other things come in and choke the Word, making it unfruitful. Others, like seed sown on good soil, hear the Word, accept it, and produce a crop-some thirty, some sixty, some a hundred times what was sown." (Mark 4:14)

May the beautiful seed that God has planted, grow in the Son, and produce a beautiful flower for the King. - P.T. Grimes

CHAPTER 2

꙰

A Seasonal Shift

"For everything there is a season,
and a time for every matter under heaven."
(Ecclesiastes 3:1, ESV)

The year 2020 began like a hot commodity for many people. I heard things like 20/20 vision, fresh starts, new beginnings, and yes, double portions of whatever you are believing God to do in your life for the year.

I hadn't really thought about a vision for the year. Normally, I would have a plan written up by New Year's Eve. But I was barely making it out of 2019 alive and with my sanity intact. To be honest, the last two years of my life were the most challenging. In fact, this was the most difficult time of my life. I felt helpless and weak.

You see, I am an unashamed daddy's girl. I grew up that way as a child, and it continued into adulthood. I am equally a momma's girl too. I have been blessed with a very strong, giving and loving mother. She has always been there for her husband and children. So, I guess I am somewhere in between. It could be because I am the last girl in the family. I sought my dad's attention all the time. He never seemed too busy or bothered by it. We have a very special bond that most girls have with their dads.

My siblings and I grew up in Miami, Florida in a community called "Overtown." To others, Overtown, Miami was considered the hood. Of course, we didn't see it that way. To us, it was home. We were a middle-class family that lived in the projects. Our household consisted of our parents and four children: two boys and two girls to be exact. We also have an older half-sister who lived a few blocks away. In a sense, we all grew up together. Our oldest sister would babysit us when mom and dad had to go out of town, which was frequently. Our childhood memories were filled with joy, fun, and laughter. Even though society would call us a statistic, growing up in Overtown, Miami taught us the value of family and community. Everyone knew each other and we were sort of the popular kids on the block. We got in trouble a lot probably out of rebellion.

Our parents were respected and yes, we were called "Preacher's kids." My dad is a preacher, and our mom didn't play! Together, they were the most feared and admired parents on the block. Every Sunday, our friends would see us dressed in our Sunday best. We had to go to Sunday school and choir rehearsal every week. We also had to go to Vacation Bible School during the summer. We low-key hated it. On Sundays, we had to sit on our plastic covered couch. Mom said she didn't want our church clothes to get dirty. In the 80's, just about everyone had plastic on their furniture. I always wondered why we never took it off because it made so much noise when we sat down!

Monday through Saturday, me and my siblings would play outside until the streetlights came on. Back in the day, the streetlight was your alarm to get your behind inside or else! Our mom would stick out her roller-covered head from her bedroom window. Then she would call all four of our names telling us "Get in this house!" Our friends would shutter with fear like her name was Mufasa or something. Then they would laugh at us sneering "Ooohh, y'all in

trouble!" We were so embarrassed. Yeah, she tried it.

My mom was respected and revered because although she was strict, she was and still is a very nurturing mother. My mom made sure we had everything we needed for school, doctor's visits, appointments, school plays and church functions. She has such a giving spirit. As I look back on my life, I don't know how she did it all with four little kids at home. My mom cooked all our meals, dressed us well, and took great care of us. She was a mother hen when it came to her kids. In our community, we were a family that most of our friends could not relate to unfortunately. It was rare to have both parents in the household. Most of our friends came from broken or single-parent homes. As kids, we didn't learn to appreciate what we had until we became adults.

My dad never let a day pass not telling my mom and my siblings that he loved us. He taught us all how to ride our bikes, drive cars, and how to fish. Dad was the carpool every school year, taking us all to school at different locations. My dad expressed his love to us in many ways. He has also been a preacher since we were young. I remember finding excuses to stay up late at night, helping him study, prepare for sermons, and asking him for help with my Sunday school lessons.

We were blessed with a great father. He has the greatest sense of humor, always joking and making us laugh. It was exceedingly rare that you saw my dad sad or upset. I never doubted my father's love for me or my family. He was always so easygoing and willing to talk things over when there was a problem. He believed in the power of communication and getting your thoughts and feelings out before they caused division. My dad is a firm believer in peace and doing everything possible to maintain it, especially when it came to our family.

Every year that passes has its share of challenges. It is how you handle them that makes the difference. My perspective on life, love, and relationships was shifting. Even my relationship with God was changing. I found myself getting angry, frustrated, and even annoyed with God. Life's hardships had become too much to bear, and I was at my wits' end. It was there, in that dark hole, that we can either push into our purpose, or like me, willingly crawl into a rabbit hole. I saw pieces of me drifting away, and I wasn't putting up much of a fight.

From someone else's vantage point, this may seem dark and depressing. But in hindsight, it was the best thing that could have ever happened to me. God was at the forefront of it all. He was stripping away the layers. He had a plan, but little did I know I was a part of it.

Two years ago, everything in my life was turned upside down. My parents and siblings were going through a travesty. I felt like I was placed in the eye of the storm. Every day I was on pins and needles cringing whenever my phone rang or whenever I received a text. My sleep was hindered by calls or being awakened in the middle of the night to horror.

I depended solely on God in this season of my life. I was

teaching and active in full-time ministry with the youth at my church. In retrospect, church became an escape from my reality. In my mind, I was trying to take care of everyone else, but no one was there to really take care of me. The worse things got at home, the more I occupied myself doing the Lord's work.

Four days out of the week were spent in church and at times, I'd come home exhausted from 12–16-hour days between work and ministry. It was in church that I could wear a mask and pretend everything was okay. But the truth was I hid the family secret no one would ever believe.

I hadn't even noticed the toll and trauma the ordeal had taken on me. My sleep was interrupted by nightmares and flashbacks. I'd hear screams as they played over and over in my head like a movie. Insomnia and I became very well acquainted during this season. Sleep would visit me sporadically three to four hours a night—if that. After a while, it left me cold and dry.

I would appreciate it if I got four to five hours of sleep a night. To me, that was progress! Still, I depended on God. He was my strength. He kept me going as I was trying to be strong for my family. Even though I was a hot mess inside, I had no other option but to keep pushing. I kept telling myself this will pass; things will get better, and I will be okay.

The fight in me was pure rage. I went to war daily in the spirit, crying out to God to make it stop! Why was my family going through this? We were always so close. We never had a problem we couldn't face together.

This time, it seemed like the more we prayed, the worse things got. I was exhausted. I felt spiritually and mentally drained from keeping everything in and bottling up my distress. It took a toll on me.

I cried to the Lord and prayed and cried until the cycle seemed redundant. I couldn't help but feel as if God was silent at one point. There I was screaming at the top of my lungs and only He could hear me. He did nothing or, at least, it seemed that way. I began to question everything. What's the point of serving and dedicating your life to God if He's just going to sit there and watch? I had always been careful not to question God and who He is, but I had some questions for Him.

Thankfully, I had sisters in Christ I could retreat to when home didn't really feel like home. We would pray; they would let me vent, and we trusted God together.

There was a season when as a family, we got desperate and started to seek the help of people we trusted from the outside.

To our surprise, those we deemed as spiritual guides let

us down. This was our burden to bear alone. It was our crosswalk. We faced challenges as a family collectively. Even more so, we faced challenges within ourselves. Blame, pointing fingers, and silent judgments had all taken their toll. It seemed as if everyone bottled their own emotions and packed them up.

Everything became a trigger. If I could offer a more vivid picture, a loaded gun sat at the table of our souls. I didn't feel safe to express my true emotions. Anxiety and uncertainty were at the forefront of my day.

Nonetheless, I continued to pray and cry out to God. It was like being stuck in a storm with torrential rain, and angry winds. I was riding the wave of my life. I did my best to seem even remotely unbothered. Faith and time became our only solace.

I kept telling myself that this too shall pass. Then a sudden shift occurred. It was as if silence could be heard in the storm. We peeked out our heads from under the covers to make sure it wasn't an illusion. As the storm began to clear, we all had to face our demons and fight the enemy within—self.

While things at home began to get better, I needed an escape. There were still battles to fight, but I found my solace in worship and praise to God. I don't know if it was my devotion to God that fueled me or if it just offered me pure distraction. I'd come home from work, lock myself in the room, and worship for two hours.

CHAPTER 3

❧

Uprooted

"And the Lord said, "If you had faith like a grain of mustard seed, you could say to this mulberry tree, 'Be uprooted and planted in the sea,' and it would obey you."

(Luke 17:6, ESV)

G oing to war in the Spirit became a militant routine for me. I didn't have to pretend I was okay. I laid it down to God every day and kept the rest of my despair to myself.

My family may have thought that I was strong inside. But there was a spiritual battle going on within me. My spirit was at war daily with the flesh. And I was tired. I wanted someone's shoulder to cry on just to release the burdens I carried for everyone.

I felt helpless and alone. But I had God. He got me through this hard season. I later moved out when the circumstances at home became too much for me. I stayed with my sister in Christ, Cynthia, who was gracious enough to let me bunker down in her dense one-bedroom apartment.

I didn't care if I had to sleep on the floor at that point. I needed my sanity and solace. I thank God how He positioned the right people in my life when I needed it.

Cynthia is the type of friend who tells it like it is. When in the spirit, she will say what thus says the Lord without any filters. Cynthia allowed me to vent to get my frustrations out. However, I prayed and asked God for direction for my own place. Going back home was no longer an option. Even though I was now traveling a longer distance to and from work, I didn't care.

Within about three weeks, I saw the hand of God shift things and grant me favor. I was able to move into my own place with a ridiculously low-down payment. I should have been expected to cough up twice the amount, but God was faithful. The agent was a believer and by the grace of God, she handed me my key.

God positioned me in the middle of the city in a high rise that could be seen miles away. On top of that, I was placed on the last floor on top, which so happened to be number seven. The building reminded me of a watchtower. You could see the entire city and various cities in between. I knew this was God. I saw things fall into place with prayer and faith. There was a lot of determination on my part. I felt a fight in me. As things began to settle down, I realized one important factor: I had a place with no furniture!

I moved in with only an air mattress, my clothes, and my two TVs. I was so anxious to be in my own space again, it didn't even hinder my move. I just trusted that God would provide. I had moved further north, and I was closer to my friends who helped me throughout this ordeal. I needed a season of peace.

Before moving, I had been spending a lot of time with my spiritual family. They had all been a breath of fresh air during my family dilemma. I enjoyed the sense of community we had. Hanging out with my sisters and brothers on the weekends became the norm. We shared a bond of being the church misfits from our previous church backgrounds.

We didn't seem to "fit in" with religion. Instead, we sought something deeper from God, a relationship. We were radicals for Jesus Christ and could not be contained.

We shared our testimonies and discovered that we all had a common thread between us. What resonated in all of us was very simple: we wanted more. Something in our spirits thirsted after more than just routine and playing church. We needed revelation and an encounter with the Most High God. All of us had experienced what we called "church hurt." We found solace in one another and were thankful to God that He had positioned us into this new place of freedom.

Freedom from religion, freedom from legalism, and freedom from depending on man to hear from God. As time passed and I began to settle into my new environment, I started to see the light at the end of the tunnel. My friends were also my spiritual family. It was me, Cynthia, Sheila and occasionally Josie because she moved to France. We would go out spontaneously. Our favorite thing to do was dance. Our go-to was listening to live reggae music at one of our favorite spots in the downtown Hollywood area.

Saturday nights, we'd all just go to release our cares and worries from that week. But every single time my sisters and I went out to party and have fun, God would intervene. We'd think it was our idea to head to a new spot or take random trips to the beach looking for hot chocolate on a cold night. However, God would always position a perfect stranger for us to minister to.

Random ministry opportunities turned into an expected occurrence whenever we went out. Another pastime we would enjoy was seeing a good movie together. The new reclining leather seats in the local movie theater were an extra perk.

CHAPTER 4

❧

Weeds

"The waters closed in over me to take my life; the deep surrounded me; weeds were wrapped about my head."

(Jonah 2:5, ESV)

O ne night, out of the blue, my girl Cynthia and I decided to see a movie. For some reason, I wanted to get all dolled up. I wanted to feel alive again. Normally, I'd just throw on sweats and a t-shirt. This time, I picked out an asymmetrical one shoulder top and a pair of skinny jeans. I got dressed and headed over to Cynthia's. She gave me a where-you-goin' look. I smiled, reading her thoughts. Cynthia always thought I was sneaking away to meet someone whenever I put a little effort into how I looked.

I realized we were going to the movies a lot later than usual. We didn't even know what to see. When we arrived, Cynthia dropped me off in the front, and I got in the line. The lines grew longer as I glanced at the movie titles and times to see what was playing.

As the line moved, my eyes noticed the most handsome man I had ever seen. I turned away, almost succumbing to the power of his gaze.

Suddenly, I felt the need to run. I stepped toward the ticket window and then realized I was in a trance. He was behind the window serving the customers. I glanced at his name tag and noticed his name was James, and he was a manager. I did a quick surveillance of his face. He was my IBM—code for ideal black man. He was my perfect type.

When Cynthia joined me in the line, I gave her the iconic sister nudge you give when you or your friend see eye candy. She glanced and nodded, signifying that he had gotten her approval as well.

As we walked in with our movie tickets, I noticed he wasn't helping the customers anymore. He had systematically made his way inside to be in my peripheral view as we walked in. That maneuver told me everything I needed to know.

The man sized me up and down and there it was. We were walking toward each other, and something told me not to make eye contact, but I ignored the warning. Contact was made and I knew I was in trouble.

Now, here's where things seemed to move in slow motion. Our eyes met as Cynthia, and I joined the roped line. The line was specifically for the movie we were seeing. His eyes held my gaze. I heard a voice whisper, "You always get scared; don't be scared."

I felt a thump in my heart that I hadn't felt in a long time. What just happened? I mean, I know I made a little effort to look nice tonight, but this felt different. I wasn't looking for anything or anyone. I was happily single and in a great place spiritually. Jesus and I were in a good place. He was my number one "boo thang." I was content.

There I was sitting in the movie theater trying to keep my mind off James. I talked Cynthia's head off about him so much she grew tired of me. The movie started, but I was in a trance again. I couldn't get that beautiful face out of my head. The way he looked at me also added fuel to the fire. I sat there as the movie watched me. Where did he come from? We had been to the movies many times, but I had never seen him before. Trust me; I would've remembered!

Then, I answered my own question and realized we were watching a late movie, which meant he worked the night shift. I hadn't seen him before because we always went to the movies early. As the movie credits appeared, Cynthia told me she needed to get her rewards card scanned so she could get points toward a free movie. I nodded, entertaining the thought of seeing James again as we exited the theater.

We walked out and alas; there he was. At this juncture, I was convinced this negro was plotting and strategically placing himself in my view. He walked across the lobby as Cynthia got his attention. His eyes gazed at my face, and I shyly looked away, avoiding his piercing, hazel eyes. We followed his lead as he made his way to the customer service desk. Cynthia attempted to make small talk with him trying to get some answers for me. I rolled my eyes at her persistent behavior. I knew Cynthia meant well, but her questions made me feel like a thirsty teenager.

Suddenly, something unexpected belted out of her mouth: "Does your wife have a husband?" she asked. I shook my head and searched his eyes for a response. They were glued to the computer screen trying to focus on scanning Cynthia's card. The light from the computer reflected on his pupils.

There, I studied the iris of his eyes. They were golden brown with a tint of green. I couldn't stop staring. He smiled and in return to Cynthia's questions said, "No, I'm not married." Before the word married could completely leave his mouth, Cynthia belted out, "girlfriend?" He said, "Nah, no girlfriend."

I was relieved as I studied the face of this beautiful man. His eyes were his best feature. They looked almost angelic with a hazel hue and the most definitively curled and long lashes I had ever seen on a man. He had butter-brown skin that glowed. His face was outlined by neatly trimmed jet-black curly hair and a smooth goatee that gave him that grown man swag.

He seemed confident and very sure of himself. This quality made him even more attractive. After he was done with Cynthia's rewards card, we left.

I knew after tonight I'd be seeing a lot of late-night movies. As I drove home, I regretted not getting his number or vice versa. I decided I'd get creative. I called the movie theater pretending I was making a complaint about the service. I said: "Can I please speak to the manager?" The worker who answered put me on hold and said the manager wasn't available. She offered to take my number and have him call me back.

If that present wasn't wrapped up with a big red bow for me, I don't know what was! So of course, I left my name and number. For effect, I added that it was urgent.

As I drove down my block, my phone rang. I answered after two rings almost dropping it on the floor of my car. On the other end, I heard a smooth, jazzy voice say, "Hi, this is the manager, James. You left a message for me to call because it was urgent. Is there a problem?" I switched up my voice to hide the hyperventilating that was happening backstage. I answered, "Oh, yes, I just wanted to call and personally thank you for assisting my friend and me tonight. We haven't experienced such customer service from anyone here for a long time." I almost busted out laughing at my poor acting skills.

He responded with "Oh, thank you! Wow, this is rare. I thought it was a complaint." He followed with, "Thank you, I appreciate you saying that very much; you made my day." I wanted to say yeah, you made mine too, but my swag wouldn't allow it.

I smirked at how creative I got trying to get him to call me. I almost heard his smile peer across the phone as he listened to my embellishments. From that night on, James and I connected and talked here and there.

Most of our chats were DM's, texts, or morning calls because of his work hours. We'd talk casually but intentionally. James took an interest in who I was. He asked questions about my work as a teacher, and he listened. He wouldn't finish work until three in the morning, so we had to get creative in our conversations.

I couldn't really read him though. There was this feeling that he presented himself one way but was guarding another side of who he was. I was sometimes confused, wondering if

I should be happy about us just getting to know each other or if I should be worried. He never rushed anything like most guys I dealt with. He seemed content with the pace we were going at, and it honestly made me fall for him more.

I knew from my past that I didn't want to start off on the wrong foot. Up until meeting James, I was perfectly fine with my singleness. My family was doing better, I was surrounded by Spirit-filled friends, and I was focused on what God had for me. For the very first time in my life, I was content with being a single woman—until now.

CHAPTER 5

❧

Planted

"He is like a tree planted by streams of water that yields its fruit
in its season, and its leaf does not wither.
In all that he does, he prospers."
(Psalm 1:3, ESV)

I went to the Lord. I lifted James before Him because I vowed not to be foolish and hasty in my next relationship. I had my fair share of heartbreaks, and I wasn't trying to become a candidate for another one. God had brought me through a lot of unauthorized relationships. I had chosen men just to feel validated or to rebound from another relationship that didn't work.

I went from setting high standards for myself and living according to God's Word to compromising my values out of fear that a man wouldn't choose or stay with me. I was done with that part of me. Or at least, I thought I was. By this time, I had been single for about four years. I'd almost forgotten how being in a relationship felt.

Relationships for me all began in stages. First, there were the beginning stages of attraction, infatuation, and then intimacy. All of that seemed foreign to me. I had trained myself not to need a man in that way. I had used God as a crutch to keep myself from healing properly. With James, I found myself afraid of falling for someone like that again. He wasn't even mine. We were just talking and getting to know each other. My thoughts raced as I attempted to brace myself for the pending heartache, I had grown immune to. It was never a case of if my heart got broken. It was when. What would I do differently? How could I turn off the insanity this time?

That's what it was. When it came to relationships, I would do the same things with different men expecting different outcomes. Before crossing over from religion to a relationship with Jesus, I would commit the most selfish sin most of us women and men do when we want something so badly.

It was simple. I wanted love. But I felt as if I had to perform for it. I told myself I had to compromise my faith and beliefs to keep a man. The climate today has become so progressive that we can sometimes become very arrogant thinking we don't need God. I was foolish to think the Holy

Spirit would partake in my sins and bad choices.

I wasn't a babe in Christ. I knew better. I knew right from wrong. On top of that, I am a PK (Preacher's Kid). But it would always come back to these series of statements with every man. "If you love me, you would..." Or "I can't wait that long." Even better, "That isn't relevant to this time." And my personal favorite, "Everybody's doing it."

Yep, it surely seemed that way. Even in the church, it seemed that Christian dating had found a loophole in compromising. Many of us Christians had a knowledge of God but neglected getting to really know Him.

In this new season of my life, God stripped me from religion and the cliché routine of playing church. After spending time operating in full-time ministry, I convinced myself that I had arrived, but God was calling me deeper. I attended an apostolic conference that my spiritual family invited me to. I encountered God's presence there like never before. For me, that was it. I had been searching and longing for an awakening like this. I wasn't getting it where I was serving. After much prayer and receiving so many confirmations that this was where God was calling me, I stepped down from my leadership position and left my church.

I wrestled with the emotional decision of leaving. I had

worked in the youth ministry, and I felt bad leaving them unexpectedly like that. But when God Himself is calling you, there is no hesitation or turning back. I thought about the countless times in scripture that the Lord called someone to pick up and leave or go to a place of the unknown.

I thought about when Jesus told His disciples in Matthew 16:24-25 "Whoever wants to be my disciple must deny themselves and take up their cross and follow Me." I wanted more than the same routine of dressing up, trying to impress others while playing church. I needed more than receiving the accolades of man.

I needed more than working like a dog to receive validation or recognition, especially from people I felt didn't even like me. All this was in the name of God. I needed to hear directly from Him. In His presence, there is the fullness of joy, and I desperately wanted that for my life.

I was so busy working in several ministries that I had forgotten that my biggest service was to spend time with God seeking His face. Sure, I was doing His work. I was serving others. But the Creator of the universe was not getting 100% from me. It was a one-sided relationship. He was giving me His all and I was giving Him a façade of service and dedication.

There He was, patiently waiting for me to realize that

spending countless hours working in ministry was just that—
works. But as it states in James 2:26, "Faith without works is
dead." I wasn't lacking in the works department. My faith
needed fine-tuning. The Lord was calling me into just that:
having a relationship with Him and abandoning religion.

As time passed, I sought the Lord more fervently
regarding my relationship with James. By this time, we spent
late nights getting to know each other. At times, he would
test the waters to see how far his flirtations could get him, but
they were slim to none. I was seasoned. I knew this game. I
had been there before, and I vowed not to fall for the same
old lines. James was open and honest about himself. He
didn't hide secrets like most men I dealt with.

One day, I wished he had kept something to himself a
little longer. James hit me with a headline. He said he didn't
want to play games with me and thought that I should know
that he was a father. James was the father of not one, but two
kids from the same woman. Great, now the infamous "baby
momma drama" came to mind.

His kids were both under the age of five. I guess James
had gotten used to women running away after he shared this
information with them. He had this big speech about
understanding if I didn't want to pursue anything further
with him.

I wanted to run away. I never wanted to be involved with a man that had a family already. I know there are many beautiful, blended families out there that make it work, but in my opinion, that wasn't exactly the ministry I was called to. I had always envisioned sharing my first child experience with my husband.

This situation made me think about things I hadn't really considered before. Would I ever have children of my own one day? What if, God forbid, some medical issue prevented me from having children? Would I be open to that? Tons of questions followed as I found myself slowly avoiding James that week. He must've sensed my distance because when I finally did return his calls, he calmly said, "Hey, stranger."

We talked about his kids and how much time he spent with them. I listened intently as he seemed genuinely happy and proud to be a father. Whenever James spoke about his kids, he lit up.

I wanted to know about his relationship with the mother of his children. I never thought I'd even be remotely close to this type of situation. I had seen and heard the drama created from failed relationships with children involved.

As an educator, I had seen firsthand the effects on both parent and child. When I asked James about his ex, he gave the typical response most men do when they really don't want to get into the details: "She's cool, but she has her days." That was enough to make me investigate further. "What do you mean "She has her days?" What is she like then?" I really wanted to ask, "Is she the crazy, jealous type?" Those thoughts were at the core, but my previous questions painted a better picture. I wanted to make sure I asked in a way that didn't cause him to get defensive or stressed by my curiosity. He surprisingly answered all my concerns and fears with ease. But now, I had another situation to consider. The man had kids and a baby momma who seasonally acted out of character depending on the weather. Great. Jesus take the wheel!

CHAPTER 6

❧

Thorns

But land that produces thorns and thistles is worthless and is in
danger of being cursed. In the end, it will be burned.

(Hebrews 6:8)

When Jesus came out wearing the crown of thorns and the purple
robe, Pilate said to them, 'Here is the man!'

(John 19:5)

I wasn't ready for this turn of events. I was just wrapping my head around the newness of allowing my heart to even feel again. This was a bit overwhelming for me, but I took my time to process it all. In my prayer time, I felt God's silence. I couldn't hear His perspective. I went to Him about James, but I was doing all of the talking instead of listening.

As I woke up one morning, I remember a dream that I had. James was in it and so were his kids. We were all together, and it looked like we were a family. The idea of becoming an instant mom scared me but my feelings for James had evolved. I honestly didn't know what we were, but

I liked the newness of it all. I liked that we took our time getting to know each other.

We technically hadn't had a date yet. His work schedule was crazy but then I started to wonder if he used his work as an excuse to keep me at bay. I was wise enough to know that when a man wants to be with you, he will find a way. I was beginning to doubt any potential we had.

My own fears about a new relationship played a big part in my doubt. I had been burned too many times to be naïve and slow. I brought up the fact that we hadn't been out together yet. Once again, his excuse was either work or his baby momma asked him to watch the kids last minute while she went out.

Now, I can vouch that most of it was true because we'd be on the phone, and I'd hear them in the background. It was always a day he had off. How strategic. He worked from the afternoon until three in the morning.

I realized that dating him would be a challenge. He also had another job in the morning. This was the downside of starting anything with a father of two. He had to work twice as hard—literally. I tried to be understanding of his situation and not become the selfish woman who wants a man to choose between her and his kids. That wouldn't be fair, and I'd lose hands down. James adored his children and I loved that about him. He didn't apologize for it.

I grew frustrated wondering how this would work. We had "the talk" and evaluated where we were and how we felt. James reassured me that he wanted to pursue things with me, but said it was hard for him to be in a committed relationship. So, there it was, my biggest fear. The truth finally came out of James and why we hadn't been able to move forward in our relationship. The whole non-committal thing brought me back to the trauma of my first love.

I compromised my faith and beliefs just because he had trust issues with women. He knew I was waiting for marriage. I had lost him because of my values, so I told myself the only way to keep him was to give him my body. I experienced the biggest hurt and pain in doing so. It was the worst mistake I had made and if I could take one thing back, it would be that. I let God down. I chose a man over Him, and I vowed never to do that again.

James revealing this to me, put me in a bad head space. I needed time away from him. I needed to process this. I went to God to vent instead of asking what He thought about the situation. My relationship with the Lord was slowly taking a back seat compared to my relationship with James. He had become an idol to me, and I didn't even notice it.

Two weeks passed before James heard from me again. I

was still angry that I had wasted so much time getting to know him and all the while, he knew he couldn't commit. "One night, during one of my monthly "girl's night sleepovers" with my friends, I woke up with James on my mind." I saw a message he left at 3 a.m. when he got off from work. His words caused my heart to feel something I had trained it all week not to feel. He apologized for withholding his truth. He mentioned that although he had gotten used to telling women that he couldn't commit, he felt something different with me and knew I wouldn't stick around had I known.

He was right. In those two weeks of being angry with him, I also missed him. I missed our talks and his flirtatious texts. I knew in my mind what I had to do but someone needed to hand that memo to my heart.

CHAPTER 7

❧

Pruning

"For before the harvest, when the blossom is over, and the flower becomes a ripening grape, he cuts off the shoots with pruning hooks, and the spreading branches he lops off and clears away."
(Isaiah 18:5, ESV)

T ime flew by and before I knew it, I was serving in ministry as a worship leader. I had found the strength to crawl back to God with my tail between my legs and repented for my distance. No matter what walk of life I was in, I knew two things: God loves me, and He is faithful, even though I had been unfaithful to Him so many times. When God called me to lead worship, I didn't feel worthy. I felt sorrow and sadness in my heart because I had deserted God during my season with James.

I repented every chance I could get. The Lord began to pour into me songs of worship and praise. I always wanted to learn how to play the piano. He even gave me the notes to play the songs breathed by the Holy Spirit. I placed each chord and lyric in my journal. Then one day, the Lord led me to sing one of the first songs He gave me to write. It was called, "New." It was such a testament of where I was spiritually and where God was calling me.

The patience of God is something I'll never understand or comprehend. I would've done away with myself and a few other people a long time ago. But God. He loves us so much. Over time, I began to enjoy my love for music and collaborating with the Holy Spirit. There was something about singing that brought me this freedom. Being in the apostolic taught me how to create a space for the Holy Spirit to come in.

There were so many beautiful moments where we could all be in various places around the world and feel the presence of God at the same time. I loved singing and worshipping God and His Son Jesus that way. There was a flow in worship.

We would invite the Holy Spirit to come in; He would lead, and we would follow. Sometimes a new song would be birthed, sometimes a prophetic word, and sometimes a word of knowledge or confirmation.

I had never experienced God like that before. Religion had limited Him to four walls. His presence was felt in and throughout us because His Spirit lives in us once we accept Jesus as our Savior. For the first time in my life, I was able to encounter and experience that truth. It wasn't something I had heard in a church service; it became my reality.

Several weeks had passed and I became engulfed with Jesus. I found strength leading worship on Sundays and even daily in my home. Our ministry was new, and we were looking for a place to have a worship service. I desperately wanted to offer my place, but it was incomplete.

I had a vision of how I wanted my home to look like and the specific furniture I wanted. I had moved out of my family's home with nothing. I was sleeping on an air mattress. There was no couch, dining room table or furniture to accommodate a worship service. I kept my brothers and sisters in Christ at bay when I moved. Even my family had not yet been in my home. I was ashamed.

CHAPTER 8

❧

Rich Soil and Mustard Seed Faith

"He said to them, 'Because of your little faith. For truly, I say to you, if you have faith like a grain of mustard seed, you will say to this mountain, "Move from here to there" and it will move, and nothing will be impossible for you.'"
(Matthew 17:20, ESV)

I dreamed of having family and friends over for fellowship and worship. I prayed and asked God to provide the furniture I desired. But it was a season of me being in a home with high ceilings and a large space. I enjoyed the acoustics as I sang to the Lord. It was just me and Him.

One evening after visiting my friend Cynthia, she walked me to my car and her face grew serious. Cynthia has a gift that she dares not boast about. She hears from God and has the gift of prophecy. She spoke many things from God over my life from the first day we met. I knew her words were not her own and were from God because everything she shared about me from our first encounter all happened and were true. I trusted it when she said the Lord had a word for me.

I didn't always like what she shared, but God would confirm the words from her lips every time.

She told me that night, the Lord said I don't have furniture because I haven't opened the doors to let anyone in. The Lord said through Cynthia, He gave me that home and it is His sanctuary. "Open your doors," He said, "and the furniture will come." I stood there and received the message.

When Cynthia left, I felt so convicted. Here I was being selfish and thinking about the aesthetic aspect of making my place a home, when God called it His sanctuary. I was both afraid and honored at the same time. I feared that I had offended God. That was never my intention. I went home and repented. Sure enough, worship rang through my home, but who was there to be blessed by it?

I knew what I had to do. That following weekend, I asked my principal if I could borrow some chairs from the school that she used for special assemblies. They were basic black fold up chairs, but they would do the job.

God had already gone before me and granted me favor. After I asked her and said it was for church in my home, she said, "Sure, get what you need." The mere thought that she said yes without asking any questions confirmed that the Lord was behind her answer. I was humbled in that moment.

The Lord wanted me to have church in my home. I took that command seriously. I prayed and consecrated my home and everything in it. I contacted my pastor and told her we could have worship in my home, and she didn't have to worry this Sunday or any other Sundays to come.

I shared my convictions with her. I wasn't taking no for an answer. For the next few weeks, worship was held in God's sanctuary. I no longer dared to call it mine. I was amazed at how instantly the Lord had blessed it. I pondered to myself at how silly I was before, not allowing people to come in because of no furniture.

God's presence was there. You could feel it when you entered. I enjoyed sharing our encounters with the Holy Spirit with my brothers and sisters in Christ. Shortly after those accounts, I purchased my bedroom furniture and my dining room table. Then later, God provided the living room suite I had patiently waited for and would not compromise on.

The word He gave Cynthia came to pass as He said. I was in awe as I remembered that prophetic word. I felt so unworthy, but I was very grateful to God for His faithfulness. I clearly remember God whispering in my ear, "I got you." He had me, indeed.

Before I knew it, the sanctuary was fully furnished and

all of it paid in full. Won't- He- do- it?! I praised God with all my might. I was thankful and elated at how He blessed me with the desires of my heart. Everything I wanted and how I envisioned it came to pass. There were still little detailed pieces I wanted, but I wasn't anxious. Little by little, the Lord strategically showed me pieces to purchase and gave me specific details of how and where to place everything. My walls were bare, and piece-by-piece God decorated my living space, His sanctuary. Time passed and I was happy. I was proud to have my family and friends over for dinner and gatherings. There was a sense of pride that swelled up in my heart. However, although I was surrounded by family and friends in the daytime, loneliness crept in at night.

CHAPTER 9

୨୧

Drought

"Her cities have become a horror, a land of drought and a desert,

a land in which no one dwells, and through which

no son of man passes."

(Jeremiah 51:43, ESV)

I only stayed in contact with James when God had a word for him, and I shared it, but he would never respond to the messages. I knew if I invited a different conversation, it would be different. He'd invite me over to see him, and I would decline. I knew what was on his mind. I ignored his foolery. I wasn't about to fall for his tricks or games.

It was my birthday weekend and one of our girls, Josie, flew into town from France. We decided to go to "Painting with a Twist" and then hang out at Dave and Busters. I wanted to be a big kid that day. The following day we decided to check out a movie. We had been going to a different theater close by my homegirl's house in the mall. That movie theater didn't have the reclining seats Cynthia and I liked. So, Cynthia appealed to go to the other movie theater.

My heart slipped into my throat. My friends didn't know how close James and I had gotten prior to our little separation. My heart raced all the way there. I'm not going to lie; part of me wanted to see James again. It had been a while. A large crowd was at the theater. I felt relieved by that, but part of me wondered if he was there.

As we walked in, everything else went in slow motion. But when I looked up, there he was. Something magnetic was pulling our eyes toward each other, and I didn't stand a chance. The man was dressed in all black and looked fine. Why Lord? Just why?

My girls and I walked past the counter where James stood. We stole glances from each other as we entered the theater. My mind was on him again. I couldn't think straight. The movie was showing but my attention only returned to it when there was a violent scene or one of my girls elbowed me with excitement in between. I suppose it was a good movie, but I couldn't tell you. The movie playing in my head won an Oscar for "Best Picture."

The picture of that beautiful man captured me. His hazel eyes and sly smile weakened all my defenses. I was doing so good without him. He was out of sight and out of mind until

I saw him. My birthday weekend celebration had been interrupted.

When the movie ended, we walked out, and Cynthia noticed she had lost an earring. I volunteered to go back to look for it. It was the perfect opportunity to stall.

I knew that I would have to face James again. Our friend Josie decided to go with me. As we walked back to the theater, my 5-inch stilettos didn't want to cooperate as I strutted up the incline near the concession stands. As I took another step, my ankle did a funky twist all the way to the floor in the opposite direction. I even heard a crackling sound, but I was so afraid of falling so I ignored it.

Thankfully, Josie caught me and broke my fall. I looked around quickly, hoping and praying that James didn't catch that embarrassing moment. I thought he was chuckling somewhere in the corner. As I got my balance, Josie asked if I was okay. I said, "Yes, but my ankle hurt." I played it down and tried to ignore the anguish I was in. We proceeded to look for Cynthia's earring. She later came in screaming that she had found it in her car.

A sigh of relief exited my mouth as I tried to hide my limp. I knew James would be at the other side of the door, so I tried to walk like Naomi Campbell, but it was hardly working. You couldn't tell me otherwise though. We walked out and of course, being the actress that I am, I made a scene with my girls right in front of James. I wanted to show him what a fun girl he missed out on. My girls and I started dancing, doing the soul train line right in the middle of the movie theater.

Everyone laughed and smiled as they passed by. I searched James' face and saw a slight grin on it. In my mind I was thinking, "Yes! Mission accomplished."

Once I was satisfied with the reaction I received from James, we left. However, I was soon brought back to reality. The worst pain trickled from my ankle and rushed throughout my whole body. Each step was painful. To make matters worse, it was my right ankle that was injured. I had to drive home using the body part I had just injured…great.

I said goodbye to everyone while slowly hopping into the car. As I drove home, I pondered on what happened. Was God giving me a warning? Why of all things and in all places did this occur?

After arriving home, I expected to see swelling around my ankle, but all I felt was pain. I grabbed an ice pack and prayed it wasn't anything serious like a sprain. I went to bed thinking about the night's events and fell asleep.

The next day was part two of my birthday weekend. I had planned a spa day to get a manicure and pedicure with my girls. As I got out of bed, I could barely walk without a limp. Every time I put weight on my right leg, it hurt. I wanted to cry. I refused to spend my birthday weekend in the E.R. so I prayed again that this would pass.

We arrived at the spa and the Asian lady doing my foot massage noticed the grimace on my face whenever she touched my ankle. I thought a massage would help but as she reclined my chair, I noticed my ankle had swollen up like a balloon! I was startled at the sight of my leg and admitted to the tech that I had injured it the night before.

I reassured her that it looked nothing like that this morning or even last night. I think my body went into shock for the first few hours because the pain and size of my ankle doubled. I stubbornly ignored it and refused to have my birthday weekend interrupted. I vowed to go to urgent care if the pain or swelling didn't subside.

After the spa, I felt proud of myself for investing in a bit of self-care. I chose my favorite color blue for my hands and feet. I love blue in any shade. This time, I went with sky-blue, and it matched perfectly with my blue baby-doll top and ripped jeans. My girls and I had dinner and enjoyed a bit of girl talk before completing our day.

I thanked God for our fellowship and sisterhood. It has gotten me through many hard times. Yet, there was one situation I wasn't ready to discuss with them because I was still trying to figure it out.

My problem had the name James attached to it. It was amazing how thoughts of him crept into the back of my mind whenever I was alone. As I returned home, I checked my phone and saw his familiar greeting from a text he sent earlier: "Good morning, Beautiful."

Now, I know this line is played and many men use it on women. So, it wasn't the text that melted me; it was imagining his voice saying it in person. In every text he sent, I could hear his smooth, slow-speaking voice reading the message aloud. It almost tingled my ears when we spoke.

I missed him but I didn't know why. What was it that I missed? He didn't want to be in a committed relationship, and I didn't want to be a friend with benefits. I was okay until I saw him.

CHAPTER 10

&

Replanted

*"Then the nations that are left all around you shall know that I
am the LORD; I have rebuilt the ruined places and replanted
that which was desolate. I am the LORD.
I have spoken, and I will do it."*
(Ezekiel 36:36, ESV)

For a few weeks, I felt strong. Freedom was rising in me
again. I wasn't distracted anymore. The Lord and I
had reconnected more deeply as I walked in my calling as a
worship leader. The Lord would wake me up at three in the
morning to give me a song of worship. His many intricate
details amazed me. Seeing this side of God made me fall
deeper in love with Him.

Our times spent together in either prayer, praise, or
worship felt like the excitement of a new relationship. The
butterflies, tingles, and anticipation of being in His presence
again gave me something to look forward to. I began to feel
like myself again. At least, the created-self God intended me

to be.

I felt as if I was betraying God just by thinking about James. He had a part of me I didn't like. He was able to hold me captive with just one look, one word, and one smile. I was in deep, deep, trouble.

Before I stopped speaking to James, I would share messages or a word the Lord gave me for him. He would never acknowledge or even comment on them. When I asked about his spiritual life, he told me he went to church regularly and was active in ministry whenever the time allowed. I was shocked because when we first met, I honestly didn't think he would even walk into a church building.

James had this pretty boy swag attached to his ego. He exuded confidence in himself without saying a word. His body language alone had you engaged in this silent conversation between two people. I wondered sometimes if the messages God gave me were for James or for me to see his unwillingness to listen or respond. Internally, I knew it was the latter, but I placed it way at the back of my mind for safekeeping.

I found myself making a lot of excuses for James. I knew he wasn't a good fit for me spiritually or emotionally. We didn't want the same things from a relationship. He couldn't even dedicate the time needed to nurture a relationship.

James had a quality that I appreciated but hated at the same time. He told me the truth about who he was, and I didn't want to accept that. Like most women, I fell into the trap of trying to convince myself he would change for me.

I should have been thankful and grateful for the information he had given me. He told me he's a father; he works long hours, doesn't want a commitment, and he indirectly showed me he and God are not that close and trust me; it wasn't because God was unwilling to meet him halfway.

The question is, what was making me pause? He clearly was the exact opposite of what I would want from a man. I prayed and asked God to take away the feelings I had for him away from me. But I knew God enough to know that my request required mutual effort.

CHAPTER 11

❧

Dry Bones, Dry Season

"Then he said to me, 'Son of man, these bones are the whole house of Israel.' Behold, they say, 'Our bones are dried up, and our hope is lost; we are indeed cut off.'"
(Ezekiel 37:11, ESV)

I knew He saw my resistance and struggling heart. If I wasn't willing to do the work, He was not going to do it for me. Deep beneath the surface, I knew that one of my battles was that sneaky, selfish, and familiar flesh.

As I said before, I had been selectively single for about four years. Before that, I had been in and out of relationships just to forget about the one before. I never gave myself time to heal. Whether it was my decision to end it, mutual, or the other party, I was tired. I felt the pain of rejection and I didn't want my self-worth to be dependent on a man.

All my friends from high school had gotten married. I grew tired of going to weddings and having my best friends' parents ask me when I was next. They acted as if I had a schedule planned for who and when I was going to get married.

I loved weddings as a kid. Early in my teens, I had my color scheme, wedding party, and guest list mapped out. But the more I attended weddings, the more people reminded me I was single. I was genuinely happy for my friends, don't get me wrong. They weren't the ones who made me feel as if I was doomed to be a spinster. It was always some random person at a wedding reception or gathering who asked me when I was getting married. It was as if they pulled a raffle and were chosen to ask me. I wanted to respond, "As soon as you stop asking me that!"

I was never the type who put myself on a biological time clock. I never had it planned that at this age I'd be married or at that age I would become a mother. I've always left that part of my life as God's business. Now, I'm not saying that I didn't have relationships that I thought were heading for marriage. I did. But they didn't work out that way.

I was secretly engaged in my early twenties and didn't say anything to my family because I knew they wouldn't approve. When the engagement was off and I ended the relationship, I was glad I saved them the trouble. I vowed not to introduce my family to anyone else until I knew from God, he was my husband.

The last serious relationship I involved them in was difficult. We had been high school sweethearts and went to college together. That ended in heartbreak after he cheated. Both my family and I suffered from the breakup. They had gotten attached to him, and we even tried over the course of ten years after that. I soon realized that you can't squeeze a sausage into a keyhole. That's what it felt like trying to resurrect our relationship.

As time passed, my friendships changed. My married friends seemed too busy to hang out like we used to. Understandably, a woman's life changes when she becomes a wife and mother. Old friendships grew apart and new friendships developed. Plus, I wasn't exactly ready to let my freedom go at this juncture of my life.

I honestly loved my independence. I liked being able to come and go as I pleased. I was able to travel, visit new places and meet new people. I was free in my relationship with the Lord and able to work in ministry whenever needed. There were those days though where I really felt alone. Sometimes, I would look at myself in the mirror and say, "You're single as hell."

Loneliness paid a visit every now and then. My body would have a mind of its own once a month. My body was like a child with a tantrum. It would fight against the Holy

Spirit with wants and desires screaming to be met. I had many nights where I'd have to put my foot down, telling my flesh, "No, go to bed hungry!"

I pondered my singleness as I sat and thought about James. I thought about how long it was since I had been in a serious relationship. Some days I just wanted someone to talk to. Other days, I just wanted someone to cuddle under a blanket and watch Netflix with on a rainy day. There were other times when I wanted someone to come home to or share how my day went. Finally, there were even days I wanted to argue with someone just to make up.

I would hear some of my married friends complain about a disagreement they were having with their husband. I'd think to myself, "At least, you have someone to fight with." Actually, I found it humorous how my married friends envied my single life. On the other side of that, here I was secretly envying their companionship.

As I thought further, I began to ask myself what many unmarried women asked. Why was I still single? Why wasn't I dating or going out to meet people intentionally? Why couldn't I be with James? Yeah, I know. I went south with that thought. But I honestly went deep into my past and compared it to where I was now.

Before my renewed relationship with the Lord, I had

been in a few committed relationships. However, they were shallow compared to what I had with Him. Jesus is simple. He wasn't interested in my religion. He showed me that religion is just too complicated; it is based on rules and striving for men. He wanted me to know what it means to be genuinely loved and accepted by Him.

On one end, my relationship with Jesus became more intimate and real. On the other end, my earthly relationships with men seemed nonexistent. I honestly felt like a nun, whatever that feels like. Frustration began to set in. I started questioning everything. Why this? Why that? Why am I still single, Lord? What else do I need to prove to You? What's wrong with me that a man can't commit? Yes, the thoughts jumped from my mind to my mouth. It turned into a one-sided conversation between me and God. I asked the questions—and then I heard silence.

I grew frustrated at this point, even with the Lord. In my early twenties, I was dedicated to Him. I had worked hard in ministry. I tried my best to be a light to all those around me. I had my battles. There were conflicts and frustrations along the way. There were also temptations of the flesh and traps from the Enemy that nearly wiped me out!

In my mid-twenties, I lived the Christian life on the fence. I slowly saw myself making compromises in relationships, and it became a pattern. I was looking for love in all the wrong places, and it cost me dearly. Sure, the Lord was right there every step of the way to pick up my mess. I began to take Him for granted. I grew arrogant in His forgiveness. I would sin and repent, sin and repent until one day, I had enough. The Lord deserved better from me. He required more from me.

This was not the life I had envisioned for myself. I went from one relationship to the next, creating the same insanity. I decided-no more! No more putting men first and God second. All through my early thirties, I remained single. There were some "potentials," but my heart wasn't ready or healed for anything new. As my thirty-fifth birthday approached, I started to heal and be content in my singleness.

The Lord had a lot of emotional and spiritual surgery to perform on my heart. I grew back in the place I've always taken for granted until now. In His Presence. That's where I found peace, love, and no insecurities or anxieties. I felt whole for the first time in my life. I didn't need a man to fill a void or anything lacking in my life. My life had purpose and I was full. Of course, with all that contentment, life has a way of throwing you an unexpected curveball. My curveball was James.

Earlier, James had left me a message that made me pause all day. It was a question he posed from our last serious conversation. We had talked about my frustrations and things not moving forward. He admitted his desire not to pursue a commitment because of where he was in his life. He worked all day with two jobs, and he had the responsibility of co-parenting two kids with his baby momma. I understood that, but then part of me couldn't.

CHAPTER 12

❧

Famine

"Our skin is hot as an oven with the burning heat of famine."
(Lamentations 5:10)

"Who shall separate us from the love of Christ? Shall trouble, or hardship, persecution, famine, nakedness, danger, or sword?"
(Romans 8:35, NIV)

I 've been there before. I knew what it is like when a man says he doesn't want a commitment. In other words, he only wants sex. I wasn't trying to hit the rewind button on my life.

I got incredibly quiet over the phone while talking to James. I was doing what I had trained myself to do to protect my heart. I did what they tell you to do when a plane is about to come down from the sky and crash: "Brace for impact." But James' question seemed genuine. It appeared to be sincere. I guess its directness made it a pivotal moment in my life. He paused for a second while collecting his thoughts.

Then he said, "Do you think you could be with a man who didn't want to be in a committed relationship right now and who wasn't as religious as you?"

Now, I know what you're thinking. That should be easy to answer with a no and an "h" to the no! But it wasn't easy to answer. I had fallen for this guy. He caused me to rethink every scenario on my list for an ideal man. He wasn't a bad person. He was honest, kind, patient, a good father, and took responsibility for his actions. Who was I to judge? I wanted to be with James so badly, but his question was loaded. I could not simplify my answer. I froze until I told James I would call him back.

I had spent half a decade committing myself to God. I never felt resentful or anxious about my singleness until now. James wasn't perfect. Obviously, he came with a lot of baggage. There were things about him that I had to reevaluate and reconsider. The difference I think with him is that he was honest. He wasn't trying to play games with me. I felt he genuinely cared about my reservations. He understood them and wasn't trying to force or pressure me into anything. That's what I told myself, at least. The whole while, I asked God to guide and direct my decisions even though I knew deep down He already did. I just didn't want to admit it to myself.

I knew that James' baggage was more than I was willing to carry, and I was not going to compromise. I had set my standards for a relationship, and I had come too far to just throw them away. But what was the tug-of-war in my heart about? Why was it so hard to let him go? I battled in my mind. My thoughts began to go left. I thought about how being in his world would affect me.

Could I stay true to my values and dedication to God? At this point, my voice of reason had left me. I reached out to him after spending the entire day processing his question. I asked if we could meet up later. This was no conversation for the phone. I needed to see him in person. I knew what I had to do, but the thought of it brought me to tears.

I had an open and honest talk with God. I laid out all my frustrations and agitations about James. I told God my truth about how I struggled between choosing His will over my flesh. I vented about how it seemed so unfair that I was walking away from another relationship that was unequally yoked. My mind understood it. My spirit understood it. Still somehow, my heart was having a temper tantrum and a fit.

I asked God for one favor. At this point in my life, I realized it was a waste of time trying to camouflage my feelings from the Lord. He knew my deepest and darkest secrets. He knows my inner thoughts even before I think them.

There was no use in pretending. God knew my struggle. He knew this one was hard. He knew I was immensely attracted to James, and I genuinely cared about him even more once I got to know him. James was different. I wasn't about to end something because he cheated, or I found out about something while someone was spilling tea.

CHAPTER 13

❦

A Protected Shell and a Lifted Veil

"He spread a cloud for a covering,
and fire to give light by night."
(Psalm 105:39, ESV)

Even to this day when Moses is read, a veil covers their hearts.
But whenever anyone turns to the Lord, the veil is taken away.
Now the Lord is the Spirit, and where the Spirit of the Lord is,
there is freedom. And we all, who with unveiled faces contemplate
the Lord's glory, are being transformed into his image with ever-
increasing glory, which comes from the Lord, who is the Spirit.
(2 Corinthians 3:15-18)

James told me everything and I trusted him. He made me feel beautiful, desired, and loved without even touching me. So, I asked. I asked the Lord for permission. I said, "Lord, this is not easy for me and it's even harder for me to ask You. But You know me in and out, and You still love me.

God, I choose You. But before I let James go indefinitely, please permit me."

Within a few seconds, I got my answer. I texted James to see if we could meet up tonight. He took forever to respond but I knew he was at work. He told me he was in another city and driving back in an hour. I grew anxious, but said, "Okay, can we meet after when you get off?"

James reluctantly said yes because he said he had to be at his other job at 6 a.m. the next day. I wasn't taking no for an answer. I ran into the shower and picked out an outfit. I felt so sad that this rare moment we would spend together alone would be our last.

My phone beeped. It was James. He told me he was home. The text that followed stopped me in my tracks: "Wear something sexy."

Boy! What is he thinking? Did he just assume because I was coming over, we'd have sex? Then as if he heard my thoughts, he followed up with, "Just kidding," with a wink.

Yeah, right bruh, good save.

As I looked at the outfit that I had chosen to wear long before his suggestive text, I realized our minds weren't that far removed. I looked at myself in the mirror and I almost didn't recognize me. The question is what was I thinking and what was I expecting from James?

I wore a black, see-through fishnet tank top with a visible black bra underneath to complement my favorite color royal blue skinny jeans and knee-high boots. My reflection talked back to me and said, "You are looking snatched!" I arrogantly responded, "Yeah, I know."

I took one last glance, a deep breath, and I was out the door. The crazy thing is that James lived only about seven minutes away from me. But tonight, it seemed like one of the longest rides I'd ever had.

I approached James' block slowly. If his neighbors saw the many times I drove around that block, they would've thought I was about to do a drive-by. In my mind, I was. Just a different kind. I was about to do a drive-by of the heart.

As I finally pulled in to parallel park, I stopped and reached for my phone. It was beeping, but I hadn't noticed because I attempted to use loud music to help ease my nerves. James had been calling me wondering what took me so long. He knew I lived a few minutes away from him, so my tardiness concerned him. I called and told him I had just parked. It was the truth, but I omitted the fact that I circled his block about six times before actually parking. I took a deep breath and sighed, "Lord, give me strength." I needed every bit of it at this point.

The environment outside James' apartment was

beautiful and had a mystic French garden feel to it. As I looked up from the bottom of the stairs, I saw him waiting for me at the top. My heart melted. We looked at each other getting one last glance before we approached. I was placing each moment in my memory bank. He looked casual as if he had just hopped out of the shower; he was wearing a white sleeveless t-shirt, long black basketball shorts, and flip flops with white socks. I laughed at myself because he looked like an ole' G. I had always seen him dressed up in all black or in professional gear for work. But no matter what he wore, the brutha looked good.

James took one step down the stairs, and I took one up. This continued as our eyes never left each other. It's a miracle that neither one of us fell and busted our butts. Everything was in slow motion, or at least that's how it felt.

Whenever James and I saw each other, every moment seemed surreal. As we were now closer, and I had one more step to take, James beat me to it and was two inches from my face. Before I could say anything, he planted the sweetest kiss on my lips. It felt so natural you would think we were together forever but this was our very first kiss!

I was elated and in despair as my senses returned to me. I had to reminded myself why I came. He greeted me with his usual, "Hey, Beautiful" and gave me a smile I couldn't resist. He grabbed my hand and helped me up the last flight of stairs. When we got to the top, he guided me in front of him. I knew he did it to check me out from behind. I smirked at the thought of it because I felt his eyes on me.

I stopped and turned around as I got to the top to let him lead the way. He opened the door for me, and it was jet black inside. I paused because I couldn't see anything, and I didn't want to embarrass myself by falling. He sensed my resistance and grabbed my hand to guide me inside. No electric lights were on, only candles everywhere. My jaw dropped. James guided me in and closed the door behind him. There was no turning back now. To ease my nervousness, I joked and said, "You didn't pay your light bill, huh?"

He smiled and returned with, "Nah, none of that, I pay my bills." Somehow, I knew he was telling the truth. James took pride in being able to provide for himself and his family. It's one of the things I liked about him.

I daydreamed many days before this. I would envision him doing just that, taking care of me. I knew if the opportunity presented itself and he had that place in his life, he would. Not because I needed him to, but I knew that was his character. James was young, but he had what older folks call an "old soul." He carried himself like those smooth mobster guys with swag. All he was missing was a cigar.

James led me to the couch and sat next to me putting his arms around me. I slid away from him playfully, but I really wanted to keep a distance and stay focused. I also wanted to get a better view of him that being right under his arm didn't provide.

The room was dark except for the dim candlelight. To add effect, it seemed as if James had summoned the moon to make a cameo for the night. There I was again—in trouble.

James and I stared at each other, smiling like a bunch of high school kids. We both seemed to be taking in the rare moment of us being alone together. Usually, his kids were around. I studied his face as he asked me how I was doing. The moon decided to creep into the large window he had at the entrance and shined on his face.

Candlelight, moonlight, it didn't matter. The man looked good in any light. My eyes traced his hazel eyes and then his long lashes. They moved to his neatly trimmed black beard and then his lips. His smile was enough to send me into orbit. I quickly snapped out of it and returned to answer when James asked me how I was doing.

I quickly answered, "I'm alright." I lied. Lord, please forgive me. I was far from all right. My heart was pounding and my mind racing. My body also turned against me and left me hanging. I glanced over at James' arms. He was wearing a white sleeveless t-shirt that brought attention to his toned and muscular physique I hadn't been able to see until now. Mesmerized by his appearance, I was into him, waist-deep like Tyrese Gibson and Meagan Good.

We sat and talked as James gently stroked my back and intertwined his hands in mine with his other hand. He talked about his kid's toys as he noticed my eyes drift to the shelves he had built for their toys and shoes. I even glanced at their beds that I could see down the hall; their bedroom door was opened.

I returned my attention to James as he talked about work after I asked how his day was. The conversation then drifted to our families and James mentioning that he is mixed. His mom is white, and his dad is black. His face lit up as he talked about his mom. He mentioned that she is still in New York where he is originally from. I asked about his dad and he said what unfortunately, most young men and women experience these days: an absentee father. He said he vowed to never be like his dad. He would always be there for his kids.

It made sense why he was so adamant about being present in his children's lives. As I listened to him talk about his love for his mother and kids, it made things more difficult. The objective behind my visit became harder and harder to fulfill.

I took a deep breath and transitioned our conversation as James finished talking about his family and after he asked about mine. I decided the best place to start was from the question he asked me earlier that made me pause. I turned my body toward him so I could look directly in his eyes. My face and demeanor grew serious as I oddly felt the presence of God giving me strength to speak my truth.

I started off by telling James that I was not a religious person as he mentioned. Now I understood the context he meant it in. I knew most people like him say that to describe someone who takes their faith in God seriously or lives in the church. I explained that I used to be that person, but the person I am now was far from religion.

James had a frown and looked confused, so I continued. I told him how I grew up in the church and was expected to because my dad is a minister, so I didn't have a choice. I told him how I had to hit rock bottom and go through hell to even begin to know Jesus personally.

I corrected James' statement and said I am done with religion. I continued that God had graduated me from religion to a real relationship with Him. James shook his head in agreement as if he understood while I broke down the difference. I explained that I wasn't the perfect goodie two shoes he made me out to be, and that I was flawed.

James responded, "Oh, okay, I respect that." I continued to answer the other part of his question about the non-committed relationship. James studied my face like a student being taught a lesson. I was surprised by his openness and willingness to hear my point of view objectively. I thought he would shut down and not want to listen. I explained to him that I had compromised myself and my faith for a man in the past who I cared about a lot. I told him it cost me everything and that I just wasn't trying to go down that road again.

I told James I wanted more. He looked at me and smiled. I let out a breath of relief, happy that I was able to get it out, but then sadness came over me. We just had a great mature conversation.

Was that it? Was I supposed to just walk out and leave? I couldn't. I remembered my petition and request from the Lord. I did my part, now it was God's turn to grant me my request. James looked at me, licking his lips, and I knew what he was thinking because I was thinking the same thing.

Before I could say anything, He grabbed my face and pulled me in for the most intense and passionate kiss I'd ever had. He was very gentle with me and not all thirsty like most guys I had encountered. Suddenly, my back started to slide to the armrest of the couch, and I knew it was time to go. James towered over me as I looked at him and told him I had to leave. I meant none of it. But I knew this was it. I had to end this. I had to end us.

We stole more kisses as we both struggled to stand up. I was weak. But God held up His bargain. I asked Him to give me just one moment with James, and I promised to let him go.

James took my hand to help me up and stared at me up and down. He hugged me and whispered in my ear, "Hmmm, lookin' all good and stuff." We were both struggling not to take it there. It was hard.

The attraction and chemistry we shared were magnetic. James kissed me again and we were out the door. He walked me down to my car, and we paused again. He held me close to him as we just looked at each other for as long as we could. I stared into his eyes trying not to cry.

This man was everything I didn't know I wanted. His sweet innocent face gave me a smile and said, "Get home safe." As we hugged again, he gave me one last kiss. I walked to the door, and James called out, "Let me know if you change your mind." I wanted to run to him at that moment, but I knew I couldn't. I drove off, trying not to look in the rear-view mirror.

CHAPTER 14

❧

Back to Eden

"And the LORD God planted a garden in Eden, in the east, and
there he put the man whom he had formed."
(Genesis 2:8, ESV)

W hen I arrived home, I went to the bathroom and
stared at my reflection in the mirror. I whispered to
myself "It's done." It was as if I had been sent on some type
of secret mission. I was still high from the sweet moments I
spent with James. It was our first time kissing or even sharing
physical touch. This night was filled with many firsts.

The irony is that what we shared was something you
would expect to encounter when a new relationship begins,
not ends. I knew that only time would get me through this
one. For now, I was happy to be on cloud nine from James'
kiss and being in his arms. It didn't feel like the end. It felt
like the beginning of something special. Is that it, Lord? Is
this how our story ends? I hoped not.

A few weeks passed and my mind pondered what James was thinking. Was he thinking about me? Did he feel what I felt? I kept checking my phone and looking for any missed calls or texts—nothing. Not hearing from James was expected. I was not surprised. He respected my wishes, especially when he knew I felt strongly about something. Whenever we had a spat, he would give me my space until I was ready to talk.

I liked the fact that James and I were able to communicate without disrespecting each other or saying things we might regret. We could talk about most things, and I missed that. I missed him. It just did not seem fair. Nothing bad happened between us, no arguments or cheating.

In the back of my mind, I knew some woman out there would be willing to be James' friend with benefits. Let's face it, the man was fine. Also, I would have been naïve to think he didn't have some type of arrangement before we met. We talked openly about those things, and I just shoved it in the back of my mind, so I wouldn't dwell on it. James knew I was different and that I wasn't that type upfront. I couldn't help but wonder if I had made a mistake. I knew the answer to that question, but my heart and flesh were pouting.

I felt God's presence almost hovering over me for the next few weeks. He felt like a mom who enters her child's room when he is asleep to make sure he is okay. I felt Him there and that brought me comfort. His silent presence was loud enough to assure me that I did the right thing.

I had to remind myself that God knows all the secret thoughts and issues hidden in my heart. He knew deep down inside I was hurting badly. I was in love with the Lord. I didn't want to hurt His heart by desiring something I knew was against His will. I was naïve to think that I could hide my true feelings from Him when He knew the truth.

Days, weeks, and then a month passed, and I was still in torment. James and I were still connected on social media. I confess that like a teenager, I would troll his page every chance I could get. At this point, it became borderline obsession. I wanted to know how he was. Was anything new or different in his life? Was his relationship with his baby momma over? I had seen a picture of her at his job with his kids.

It was no mystery who took the picture. Insecurity and jealousy crept in. This was my only connection to him. The only way I could see him without really seeing him. Here I was playing all kinds of scenarios in my head and the man wasn't even mine. I let him go. But did I?

Many days I would attempt to send a DM and then I'd erase it. I wanted to call or text him, but I knew he would draw me again with his smoothness.

I barely spent time with my girls. I was so consumed with James that I couldn't even remember the last time I had seen them. I missed them, but I didn't want them to see me in the state I was in. My laundry had piled up, my home got lost under total chaos. All I had the strength to do was get up, go to the bathroom, shower, and repeat. I slept in a lot at this point. Sleep was the only way I didn't feel the pain. I eventually realized I was mourning. I was grieving the death of our relationship.

I couldn't tell you how many times I cried myself to sleep. When I woke up in the mornings, my eyes were synonymous with Rocky Balboa after a beat down. They were swollen and tired. I dealt with my pain in silence. I dusted off all my breakup songs and used them to lick my wounds.

I had that song, "Nobody Knows" by Tony Rich on repeat. It seemed to sum up perfectly how I felt even though I was the one who said it was over. I guess I was hoping there was the slightest chance he would reconsider and give us a chance.

I had been here before. I knew better. If there were still women out there willing to give men themselves without requiring a commitment, then why should they settle down? I cried out to God asking Him when it would stop hurting. I knew my cycle. I knew this pain all too well. I decided that I'd adopt Toni Braxton's title from the 90's, "The Diva of Despair." Yep, that was me. I owned it and I wore the tiara with grace.

After another week of torment, I couldn't take it anymore. I decided to reach out to James to see where his head was at. I asked him how he was doing via text. He responded a few minutes later with an excited, "Hey, Beautiful!" I hated that he called me that still. It was like taking a bullet to the heart. He asked how I was and returned that he was doing well. I couldn't bring myself to ask what he'd been up to.

Part of me didn't want to know. James had a way of poking holes into my flesh with his flirtatious remarks. He had the audacity to ask if I wanted to stop by after he got off. Did he not listen to anything I had said? The invitation alone was tempting. But I knew where that would end.

James respected my wishes, but it didn't mean he would give up trying once he had my attention. I quickly ended the conversation knowing where it was headed if one of us wasn't strong enough. I knew this was no man's land. Either I let him go or succumb to my flesh. There was no middle or in-between solution here.

The next morning while still in bed, my thoughts ran

straight to James. My mind began to ponder. I got flashbacks of our last encounter together. I admit it was intense, sexy, and tempting. I replayed it over and over in my head until suddenly, I heard a voice say, "Did God really tell you not to be with him? Is it really a sin to have sex before marriage? It says don't be unequally yoked with unbelievers. But James is a believer."

The voice continued: "You have been faithful to God. You have been single for such a long time. He created you with these feelings and emotions. So, aren't you supposed to acknowledge them? How is it fair that you have to suffer and ignore the natural needs and cravings of your body?"

I was fully aware who was talking to me, and it wasn't God. I knew it was the voice of a stranger. I knew it was the Enemy but no matter how hard I fought it, I agreed with him. Resentment built up in me toward God. Why would He make me give up the man I had fallen for and had a good relationship with? Why do I always have to choose?

It always boils down to a man or God? Why can't it be both? Why one or the other?

That seed planted by the Enemy started to take root. I grew angry and hurt began to blindside the goodness of God. After the one-sided talk, I pictured Eve in the garden. I realized that I, like so many other women, had been hard on her.

I remembered thinking, *so that's what it was like for her*. I felt the tug-of-war she experienced between wanting to obey God her Creator and the intense desire to satisfy her flesh. I sympathized with her struggle to resist her fleshly desires as the serpent painted such a mouthwatering picture. I saw first-hand how he took God's word and twisted it to seem like you didn't really understand what God meant.

With determination, I started searching scripture looking for an indefinite verse that justified my resistance. Although I knew what the Bible said about keeping the marriage bed undefiled and not committing sexual immortality, my mind decided that a handy dose of selective amnesia would suffice.

Nonetheless, my flesh and heart couldn't hear of it. Since I couldn't be with James in the natural, I convinced myself that my hidden fantasies wouldn't be interrupted. I continued to troll James on social media and even played detective to get to the bottom of his relationship with his baby momma.

That picture of her at his job ruined the last part of me that was left. I did what most women did. I went undercover cop, surveillance, and FBI Agent on her. By this time, I was long gone. I had exited stage left. My pain had morphed into pure obsession and insanity. I couldn't rationalize my thoughts. I would hear God's whispers, "What are you doing?" But I just ignored Him.

I felt let down by God. I attributed Him to a mean father telling his daughter she can't see this guy he didn't approve of. As far as I was concerned, James was a nice guy. But I knew what he wanted from me was non-negotiable to God. The Lord was being protective of me, and I knew it. I didn't like it, but I knew it.

I discontinued talking to James because his requests for me to come "visit" started to taint my mind. He drew me in inconspicuously. He had a way with words that made you ponder and freeze. I decided that if I couldn't have him physically, I would in my mind. It was like binge watching my favorite TV shows on Netflix. The playbacks of our encounter were on repeat.

I pondered in my head the question that I shouldn't ask. What if I didn't leave James' apartment that night? What would've happened? Would I have been strong enough to resist the temptation? Would I be another chick who succumbed to another pretty boy? I knew it was a rhetorical question, but I still asked. I hated the fact that I was acting like a schoolgirl with a broken heart.

Even worse, I opened the door to my mind to go places it didn't need to go. I felt like I was slowly crawling into a rabbit hole that nobody could get me out of. I was too ashamed to pray. I knew God was disappointed at my choices. I also knew that in God's eyes, thinking, lusting, and fantasizing about James was no different from being with him physically. At that point, I didn't expect His goodness and mercy. The Enemy had set me up to fail. To add insult to injury, he quickly flipped the script and became my accuser, requesting my soul. My mind was fully invested in the rebellion of my heart.

One day, I had gone too far. My thoughts became a reality in my dreams and sleep. My sexual desires had been awakened and I felt ashamed. I knew this behavior was just a quick fix to my pain. I had no outlet. Guilt and shame made me too embarrassed to talk to my family and friends about it.

There was no way I was going to subject myself to judgment. I was harder on myself than anyone, so I had the judge and jury down pat. I felt like I was having an adulterous affair. Others with a natural mindset might say, "What's the big deal? Having fantasies and thoughts are normal." Yeah, but I knew better.

I knew that with any sin, whether stealing, killing, committing adultery or fornication, it all begins with a thought. The mind is the nucleus of every decision we make.

The fact that I allowed my mind to go so deep that even my body felt like I was with James was not good. It was all the Enemy needed to get me to bite the bait. I had no fight in me. Condemnation, guilt, and pain had taken their toll on me. It's one thing to correct a child who has a first offense and didn't know better. But how would God forgive me for this? He had forgiven me so many times before. I didn't feel worthy of forgiveness this time. I felt as if God had given up on me. I was angry at Him, and I knew He felt my anger. I felt that my Christian walk brought me nothing but restraint and loneliness.

I knew God heard my thoughts, and I hurt His heart. The crazy part about entering a relationship with the Lord is that you even start hearing His heart. Even in silence, I felt Him. But it was me and my shame that put a space between us.

The Enemy is very strategic because he knows that sin separates us from God. Jesus came to the earth to mend and restore the relationship between God and His children. I knew also that Jesus paid the ultimate price so that nothing could separate me from the love of God. No one except me. I knew God loved me. I just couldn't accept that truth through the eyes of guilt. I had let Him down again and wasn't ready to face my fears.

CHAPTER 15

❧

The Lion, Snake, and the Gardener

"This is what God told me: 'Like a lion, king of the beasts, that gnaws and chews and worries its prey, not fazed in the least by a bunch of shepherds who arrive to chase it off, so, God-of-the-Angel-Armies comes down to fight on Mount Zion, to make war from its heights. And like a huge eagle hovering in the sky, God-of-the-Angel-Armies protects Jerusalem. I'll protect and rescue it. Yes, I'll hover and deliver."

(Isaiah 31:4-5, MSG)

The following day, my girls and I decided to hang out after worship. There was a carnival in town, and we decided to check it out. As we were walking, we admired the natural beauty around us. People walked in the middle of a paved pathway. To the right of us was the carnival and on the left was a beautiful grassland area.

I admired the beauty as we walked along the pathway. It was serene. Suddenly, I saw a huge lion emerge from the grassland field! His eyes were fixed on me. I don't know if I was in shock or what, but I wasn't afraid. He walked directly toward me.

For some reason, I was still. I wasn't running or screaming. I noticed that he was bruised and had a deep scar on his right side. The lion looked exhausted as if he had been in a battle. As the lion continued to walk in front of me, he stared deep into my eyes. His eyes expressed a mixture of sadness and love. He looked down and then spat out something that was clutched in his jaws.

As he did so, I looked, and it was a snake! The snake was green and missing its entire body! There was only a head, and it was still alive! *How was this possible?* I thought. The head of the snake began to gnaw and attack on the ground as it slithered even without a body.

In fear, everyone in the crowd started running and screaming. As I looked up, I noticed it was approaching my friend Sheila. I screamed, "Sheila, watch out!" The snake turned its head and then headed toward me. It had opened its jaws wide and started to pursue me.

I ran away and tripped into the crowd of people. I was still on the ground. In despair, I looked up and saw the snake right in my face. Its jaws were inches away. Its color was jade green and fangs long and sharp. Its mouth was full of saliva.

I had never seen anything so repulsive.

As I looked around for help, I noticed that the lion had taken a place on the sidelines. He was standing right next to my friends Cynthia and Josie. I didn't have time to pause or ponder why my friends or the friendly lion didn't seem interested in helping me.

It seemed that this battle was mine alone. Where did this tamed lion come from? Why was he acting like he knew us? More importantly, why didn't he finish this snake off? I was face-to-face with this snake. I tried with all my might to get up, but I couldn't move. My body was stuck to the ground. In an instant, I felt the wind blow. Something told me to open my mouth and I began to pray in the Spirit.

It was like tongues of fire as I felt my strength return to me, and I was able to sit up. Before I could notice anything, my dad appeared out of nowhere wearing all white. He stomped his heel right on top of the snake's head, crushing its skull to the ground.

There it lay, lifeless. Next, my dad pulled out one of his white handkerchiefs. He covered the snake's head and flung it into the grasslands. He helped me up and said to me, "In order to kill a snake, you always go for the head." He smiled at me and hugged me. I squeezed him in relief. He saved my life.

It was the first time in two years that I had seen my father as a hero. He saved the day. As I turned around to look for my friends and the lion, my eyes flew open. My body flung up. Oh my gosh! It was a dream!

I sat up in my bed, staring at the walls. I had never had such a vivid dream. I knew this wasn't just another dream. It had a meaning and served a purpose. I closed my eyes to recapture the key characters in the dream. It was as if I was in a movie instead. The players that stood out were the lion, the snake, and my dad. As I pondered the roles each character played, I felt the Holy Spirit paint an accurate description of what the dream meant. I shoved the thought into the back of mind. It was too overwhelming.

As weeks passed, work became a distraction for me. I had been working long hours just to stop thinking about James. I had saved my thoughts of him for after hours and late at night. One day, while at work, I noticed a missed call from Cynthia.

It had been weeks since I had seen her, and I knew I couldn't face her now. I ignored her call and then I saw she had left me a voice message. One thing I knew about Cynthia was that she was very persistent when she wanted to reach you. I listened to her message after work. It said: "Hi, it's Cynthia. I need to share something important with you.

I have a word for you from the Lord, and I need to share it with you in person, not over the phone." My body shook. Whenever Cynthia said she had a "word from the Lord," I knew it was something serious.

The prophetic gift God gave Cynthia made me afraid of her when we first met. The Lord had used her to tell all our business at a women's retreat in Orlando, Florida a few years back. Every single time she said she had a word from the Lord, I knew it to be true. When I would go to God myself for accuracy, He would always confirm it. I also knew that in Scripture, whenever God sent His prophet to someone, it was to speak over you, expose something you tried to cover up, or to warn of pending judgment.

I became anxious and afraid just thinking about what the Lord shared with Cynthia. Thank God for Jesus and that He spared us from condemnation. But that didn't mean I wouldn't pay for my sins. It didn't mean I wouldn't be held accountable for my shortcomings. I was afraid of what would be shared. My anxiety wouldn't let me wait.

I showed up at Cynthia's apartment later that evening after work. I approached her door and took a deep breath before knocking. Cynthia greeted me with a hug and a solemn smile. Her face looked focused as if she had been spending time with God all day. She seemed profoundly serious, and I grew more anxious.

She invited me in to sit and asked if we could pray before she began. She asked for God to come in and speak through her. I watched as my friend beckoned to God. She asked that nothing she said would come from her and that everything she spoke would come from the Lord alone. She also prayed and said, "Lord, if anything is from me, may it fall to the ground and die."

I sat up straight to brace myself and listened. Cynthia began with a dream she had. My first thought was the dream I had days before. I thought to myself, *"Now she's having a dream?"*

I knew this wasn't a coincidence. She described her dream. She said she and I were in a classroom doing an assignment she didn't understand. She continued that she was asking me for help but couldn't get my attention. She said I was distracted, and I ignored her as she called out my name several times.

Cynthia said I got out of my seat and started running after something. She started chasing after me, but my focus was on whatever I was chasing. According to her, I was wearing all white. I was riding on a chariot chasing a woman. She couldn't make out the woman but I was completely distracted and eager to chase her.

Cynthia said she shouted my name from the top of her lungs, but I couldn't hear her. I was totally absorbed in pursuing this woman. "It was almost obsessive," she said. When Cynthia made that comment, it didn't take much for me to figure out who I was chasing. I knew it was James' ex. I had been trolling her on social media trying to get to the bottom of her relationship with James.

My focus returned to Cynthia as she paused in her description of the woman I was chasing. Her eyes grew large as she stopped and looked at me and asked, *"Who is this woman?"* She asked it rhetorically, but because of my convictions, it sounded like a direct question she needed me to answer. I quickly swallowed the toad in my throat as her eyes searched my face. It was as if my eyes gave it away, but she didn't say anything.

Cynthia said that was the end of her dream. She stated she didn't understand its meaning and asked God for clarity. She explained that night, she went to sleep, and the Lord woke her up around 3 a.m. She recalled the Lord's voice and tone startling her so much her eyes fluttered open. She answered the Lord's call and sat up in her bed shaking, "Yes, Lord, I'm awake."

Cynthia said the Lord continued in a thunderous voice saying, "Tell Pam to leave him alone!"

On hearing that she asked, "Leave who alone, Lord?" Instantly, I looked up at Cynthia in fear. She stood up slowly and stared into my eyes. It was as if the Lord Himself had possessed her body. Her eyes grew large as her voice growled the name, *"James!"*

I closed my eyes in horror and pure conviction. There was nothing I could say to defend myself. How do you argue with an all-seeing, all-knowing God? I sat there in tears as Cynthia apologized for the message she had to deliver. She knew it hurt me. But I thanked her and stood up. I headed for the door fighting back tears.

I walked to my car under the bright full moon. It appeared to have been strategically positioned to walk me to my car. I looked up at the moon with a silent nod of gratitude. I also remembered the last time I had seen a moon so bright. It was the last time I saw James. Everything came full circle now. It was almost poetic. A perfect moonlight the night I decided to say goodbye physically to James and a perfect moonlight when God finalized it.

While driving in my car, I felt nothing but fear and trembling toward God. The flashbacks of Cynthia's face and eyes when she reiterated God's words shook me. I had offended Him. I had done more than a physical act could. I betrayed God emotionally with my heart. James and his ex had become idols in my insanity, and I was the last one to notice.

I pondered on the dream Cynthia had and saw a visual of myself behaving like a mad dog as she described. I reflected on the part of her dream where I, dressed in all white, was chasing a woman on a chariot. That puzzled me. Why the chariot? Why white?

As Cynthia pondered the same, she mentioned the fact that white usually represents something good. But obviously, this dream wasn't. I recalled the white handkerchief. What was the correlation there? I wasn't sure, but I knew somehow, they were connected.

As I drove home, I couldn't help but reflect on Cynthia's face after she announced James' name. I knew I couldn't conjure up any fancy or spiritual words to get the Lord's attention. Even though I felt like my words weren't going past the ceiling, I was in the exact position God wanted me, completely broken.

It is what He requires from all of us when we fall. Unfortunately, I didn't get the memo until much later. I realized and understood better what King David meant in Psalm 51:16-17: "For you do not delight in sacrifice, or I would bring it; You take no pleasure in burnt offerings. The sacrifices of God are a broken spirit; a broken spirit and a contrite heart, O God you do not despise."

That's when things got real for me. In that very moment, I realized God didn't want my blood or an emotional performance. All He required from me was a broken and contrite spirit.

I pulled up to my home and was determined to get clarity. I had to ask the Holy Spirit to interpret the dream. Once I entered my apartment, I dropped straight to the floor and lay down prostrate before the Lord. Within seconds, I was on my face in tears. The mere thought of being separated from the Lord in any way brought on pure anxiety. I repented and asked His forgiveness. I knew I had offended Him. The fear of the Lord returned to me in that instant.

I don't know how long I'd been lying there. It must've been a few hours because the sun started to make its appearance in the sky. I picked myself up off the floor slowly and headed to the edge of my bed. I sat in silence knowing that the Master had my attention, and I had His.

Immediately, I saw a flash come before me. It was the dream I had about the lion, the snake, and my father. The only difference between the dream and what was happening right there is that I was fully awake! It was a vision right before my very eyes! Suddenly, I heard a still, quiet, and familiar voice. It was the Lord! I can't tell you how comforting it was just to hear His voice again. I felt so unworthy of His presence.

As I listened closely, He said: "I am going to show you what your dream meant. The Lion you saw was Jesus. He had a scar on Him because He was in battle. The Lion of Judah was fighting on your behalf. The snake represented James. Jesus saw the snake setting traps for you. My Son was fighting on your behalf. Jesus could have finished the snake off Himself, but I needed to expose and reveal the Enemy to you in his true form. You needed to see for yourself what you were up against.

The Enemy had you blinded and deceived you. He masked himself behind the guise of a handsome, young man. His true nature was represented in your dream. Green with envy, filled with the saliva of demons and crawling like the curse he is. When the Lion (Jesus) dropped the snake out of His mouth, that was the opportunity I was giving you to have a face-off with the Enemy.

I equipped you with my Word and Spirit. That is why (Jesus) the Lion went on the sidelines with your friends, Cynthia and Josie. It seemed as if they were doing nothing, but they were interceding for you in prayer. You were blinded, daughter. You had everything at your disposal to defeat the snake (the Enemy). But instead, you ran away in fear. You forgot who you were and who I created you to be. Next, you fell to the ground and were positioned face-to-face with the snake. That should never happen! My seed must never be on the same level as the Enemy.

The serpent was cursed to the ground. My Son died so that the Enemy stays under your feet! Being at eye level with the Enemy shows how far you had fallen and gotten away from My presence. When you felt the wind and the urge to pray, that was the Comforter, the Helper beckoning and warring in the Spirit for you. That is why you heard yourself praying in tongues. The Holy Spirit was making intercession for you. You forgot who you are. You are My child, and you have My Spirit living in you. You needed to use the spiritual weapons I have given you to fight against the Enemy.

Finally, when your dad appeared, he stomped on the snake's head and defeated him. Your earthly father was a representation of Me. I am your heavenly Father. I came in to finish the job. The white handkerchief that your earthly father had to cover the snake's head was to represent protection. I am your protective covering.

Your earthly father is your spiritual covering on the earth. The white handkerchief represented Me coming in to cleanse, heal, and set you free. You were wearing white in Cynthia's dream to represent the price Jesus paid for you.

Yet, you were going in the complete opposite direction of what His blood was shed for. He was wounded for your transgressions. He was bruised for your iniquity. Now you know. You now see and know the love I have for you, daughter. I will go to war for you. Jesus is the one who has ransomed you. He is your bridegroom."

After that, I was stunned. No words could describe the depth and intensity of the Father's love for me. It was clearly displayed to me in that dream. I was overwhelmingly grateful. The Enemy lost the battle for my heart. He lost badly. The Trinity showed up with a strategy to win me back. The love of God was displayed with such intentionality.

I could never doubt the veracity of that again. I will never forget this moment for the rest of my life. It's an encounter embedded into my soul.

A week after the Lord interpreted the dream for me, He led me to go to the store to finalize the decorum for my home. One empty space remained in my dining room that I had not covered. I went to Ross one day and prayed, "Lord, show me which one?"

He guided me down a back aisle and said, "That one!" I looked at the painting on the shelf and grabbed it quickly. I studied the large canvas and tears flooded my eyes. It was a painting of a large lion's face adorned with Afrocentric detail.

The lion had a crown in the form of animal skin. He had a scar under his eye and a snakehead was at the bottom of the canvas. Remarkably, I didn't even notice the snake until the Lord disclosed it to me a few days later!

The Lord is a detailed and intentional God. He was teaching me how to depend on Him in every aspect of my life. Whenever I look at the painting in my home, it is a constant reminder of the Lord's goodness and mercy. It also reminds me of how He rescued me like a superhero in that beautiful and prophetic dream.

The Lion and the Snake canvas the Lord led me to purchase to complete
my home as a constant reminder of the prophetic dream I had.

CHAPTER 16

❧

The Farmer Returns

"My friends, be patient until the Lord returns. Think of the
farmers who wait patiently for the spring and summer rains
to make their valuable crops grow."

(James 5:7, ESV)

I saw justice pleading its case against me. I could hear the Enemy demanding my life before the throne of God. Satan had presented his evidence; he gave the jury ulterior motive on my part. He failed to mention that he had planted the seeds in my head, but I knew that was his character. I saw him in his pure form: 'The Accuser of the brethren."

I wanted to present my cuffed hands before the Lord who was the Judge. As I looked up to Him with tear-filled eyes, I saw a beautiful man approach the bench with a file folder. He looked like a lawyer and said to the Judge; "I have evidence that the accuser omitted from the people's evidence folder. I gave him this report a long time ago, Your Honor. It is the same evidence from other cases I've represented.

The prosecution has brought before you, very incompetent, and redundant accusations against my clients. He has failed to include in this case the vile, deceptive, and manipulative ways he has trumped charges against your people. He has selective hearing and memory, Your Honor," the lawyer said as He winked at me with a smile.

I smirked at His comment and wondered why he was defending a stranger. He doesn't even know me! I thought. As I looked up at the Judge, He raised His gavel and yelled: "Case dismissed!" He continued, "The evidence shows here blood that was rendered in the defense of this client. Your accusations are null and void. She is free to go." I looked over at the accuser as he threw away the files that contained evidence of a crucified and resurrected Jesus.

Jesus paid the debt for me. The accuser sat and sulked in defeat as he knew there was nothing he could do. The lawyer continued, "Your Honor, if it's all the same to you, I would like to file a motion for the prosecution to be held in contempt of this court. He brought charges against my client but failed to read her rights and did not grant her the right to be represented by her attorney." The Judge gave the accuser a growling stare and returned his eyes to the lawyer. He responded, "So ordered. Bailiff, take him away!"

In shock and awe, my mouth flew open! What just

happened here? Who was this man who came out of nowhere to defend me? Was I dreaming again?

Nope, I was wide awake! It was a vision! Yet again, God was showing me His grace and mercy. My lawyer was Jesus, the Judge was clearly God, and the prosecution was obviously the Enemy. I fell on my face and worshipped the Lord. I knew I was guilty. I knew I had sinned. My eyes were blinded by tears as the song, "Mercy Said No" by CeCe Winans came to mind. Justice was in the right to ask for my soul. But at that moment, for the very first time in my Christian walk with the Lord, I deeply appreciated and saw the power and validity of the blood of Jesus.

No sin I commit can keep me from His grace. I no longer take that for granted. When God Himself could have rightfully ended my life, Jesus' payment for sin justified me. In a court where the keys were thrown at me, I was made right with God through Jesus, my defense attorney. It painted a picture so clear for me.

As a child, I would hear my grandmother, mom, and dad speak about the blood of Jesus. But in my adolescent, teen, and young adult life, I took it for granted. The courtroom in the kingdom of God vindicated me. The blood of Jesus has real value! It overrules all the Enemy's accusations against me.

I realized I am free! But God needed to remind me of the cost of that freedom. My journey was just beginning. God had to hit the restart button on my life. We needed to revamp and reevaluate our relationship and how we got here—more so, how I got here.

God had never left or deserted me even though it felt as if He did. That's the cost of free will. We want freedom. However, as 1 Peter 2:16 states, we must "Live in freedom, but do not use your freedom as a cover up for evil, live as servants of God." I had to realize a high price was paid for my freedom. I never want to make light of that again.

CHAPTER 17

❧

Blossoming and Becoming

"The fig tree forms its early fruit; the blossoming vines spread
their fragrance. Arise, come, my darling,
my beautiful one, come with me."
(Song of Songs 2:13)

S everal things needed to take place in my life from here on out. I made a conscious decision to rededicate my life to the Lord. I couldn't do things as I did before. I felt led to disconnect with everything that distracted me from God. I was adamant about positioning myself to hear from Him more clearly.

I made the mistake of thinking that my deeds alone helped in working out my salvation. "I was broken." I desperately needed God's Spirit to do the work in me. I had to understand that God didn't need my assistance to heal my brokenness. He just needed my willingness to submit to His will and allow Him to be Lord over my life.

Learning how to depend on God alone was not going to

be an easy task. A lot of dying to *self* was required. My independent thinking had to be thrown out the door. I was used to being in control of my life. I dictated how and when I would position myself to hear from the Lord. However, my one-dimensional thinking needed to change.

I had to die to self. I needed to surrender the innermost parts of me to God, even the parts of me I thought I was hiding from Him. Yeah, I was naïve and arrogant to think that God wasn't aware of my issues. He was well-aware. He was more aware than I was. Who did I think I was fooling? How did I get to this place?

I thought the Creator of the universe wasn't privy to my emotional distress. I believed that He was only concerned with how I served in ministry and not the desires of my heart. I would easily believe God for someone else. The problem in my thinking was believing God would do the same for me. I had trust issues that went beyond my issues with men and relationships. My trust issue was with God.

It was November into the end of December 2018, that I had gone through the whole shebang with James. A new year was approaching. I felt led by the Lord to leave everything behind in 2018. I was not about to bring my old mentality into 2019. I needed to surrender and lay aside everything that pulled my attention away from God.

I set out a plan to weed out the things that distracted me. The Lord gave me a list of items that needed to go asap. The first thing I had to let go was social media. I deactivated all my social media accounts. There was no logging off temporarily. They needed to be uprooted. It was the main culprit of my distraction and interactions with James. This was a hard task to follow through with, but I was determined.

The second thing I was led to do was to go on a sabbatical. I had reached out to my pastor and explained to her the crosswalk I was on. I stepped down as worship leader for a season until my worship became an intimate dance between me and Jesus.

The Scripture where a rich man asks Jesus what he must do to be saved came to mind. Jesus told him to go and get rid of all his possessions and follow Him. The rich man walked away because he wasn't willing to let go of the things he held precious. But notice, Jesus didn't chase after him.

Jesus needed me to prioritize Him and recognize He is everything I need. I had to be willing to let go of my idols. Without even realizing it, I had several idols that had made their way into my life. As God began to pour into me, He identified them one by one. Guilt flooded my heart as I repented for each one and laid them down at His feet. For sure, James had become an idol in my life. He was my first thought in the morning and my last at night. My mind and heart had been enslaved.

My every thought, motive, and desire had been dictated by my interactions with James. The sad part is he was totally oblivious of the hold he had on me. But then again, it wasn't him operating. James wasn't perfect but he was a tool the Enemy used to distract and draw me away from my relationship with God. Of course! That was it! The Enemy's entire scheme throughout history is and was to separate us from God.

The Enemy knew the only way we could be separated from the Lord is through sin. Sin is also accomplished through free will because God will never force us into a relationship with Him. His goal and the intention of the cross were to settle the score with the Enemy and reconcile our relationship with Him as He designed in the garden of Eden.

I revisited the book of Genesis to investigate God's original purpose and how the Enemy tricked and manipulated Adam and Eve into sin. Genesis Chapter 1:26 says, "Then God said, let us make mankind in our image, in our likeness." Verse 27 states, "In the image of God he created them; male and female."

It continues in Genesis 2:7: "Then the LORD formed man from the dust of the ground and breathed into his nostrils the breath of life, and the man became a living being." So here I saw how God was intentional in creating us in His image. Later in Genesis 2:16, God gives Adam a directive.

He says, "You are free to eat from any tree in the garden; but you must not eat from the tree of the knowledge of good and evil, for when you eat from it you will certainly die." There it was. God had given Adam a clear command. So why did he disobey Him?

CHAPTER 18

✣

Revisiting the Garden

"So then, I have to insist that in the Lord, neither is woman inferior to man nor is man inferior to woman. For just as woman was taken from the side of man, in the same way man is taken from the womb of woman. God, as the source of all things, designed it this way."

(1 Corinthians 11:11-12)

As an educator, I can remember the countless times I instructed my students to walk in the line and they ended up falling and hurting themselves. Why? Because they chose to ignore my rules and decided that running was better and got them to where they were going faster. I can think of many other times when my students disobeyed my instructions and ended up in scenarios that brought them more harm than good. Isn't that just like a child you tell not to do something, and he does it anyway? Perhaps, like Adam, all of us have been like my students when it came to God's instructions. But I wanted to search deeper. I continued reading and discovered something most interesting. Adam lived in the garden alone for some time. He only had the animals for company. God gave Adam the rule over everything. However, God saw that Adam still didn't have a suitable helper for him. That's when God created Eve. She was birthed in reverse because God created her from Adam's rib. She was a part of him.

Chapter 2:25 is very intriguing when it states: "Adam and his wife were both naked, and they felt no shame." That stood out to me because from the moment I realized I had sinned; my first instinct was to hide. I felt ashamed. But before Adam and Eve sinned or disobeyed God, they felt no shame.

Isn't that the place God intended and still intends for us today? To be free and naked before the Lord without guilt or shame? That was the first revelation I got in my quest to debunk Satan's tactics. He knows that sin produces shame. It makes us look at ourselves instead of keeping our eyes on God. The second tactic of the Enemy I saw is found in Genesis 3:1: "Now the serpent was craftier than any of the wild animals the LORD God had made. He said to the woman, 'Did God really say, you must not eat from any tree in the garden?'"

I had to stop right there! That is the exact line he fed me

while trying to get me to disobey God's instructions not to have sex before marriage. He fed me with that same crap! Verbatim! "Did God really say?" Humph! That is Satan's second tactic—getting you to doubt God's Word or to disobey Him. Jesus gives us a perfect example of how we should combat the Enemy when he tries to get us to disobey the Word of God.

We find it in Matthew 4:1 after Jesus had been led into the wilderness and fasted for forty days. Satan always comes at us with the mundane questions before he strikes. He attacks the mind to make you think you heard wrong. He even had the audacity to approach the Son of God with his mess! But Jesus, in His humility knew the price He willingly decided to pay for humanity.

Jesus understood His assignment. He understood that He had to become like us and face the same temptations we face to authentically justify us. Once again, Satan starts off his manipulations with a sense of reasonable doubt. "If you are the Son of God, tell these stones to become bread." Here, Satan tempts Jesus in the same strategic way that he tempts us. He approached Jesus at a point of weakness. Satan knew that Jesus was hungry because He had been fasting for forty days.

Isn't that just like the Enemy? He tempts us in our

moments of weaknesses. But I love Jesus' response in Matthew 4:4. He says, "It is written: Man shall not live on bread alone, but on every word that comes from the mouth of God." I believe that Jesus' intention of even entertaining the Devil was to give us a blueprint on how to handle Satan's devices.

I honestly believe He came to rectify what happened in the Garden of Eden. Had Adam and Eve only applied the Word they received from the Lord; this deception would not have taken place. But God, in His infinite wisdom, knew the fall would've taken place. Just like He knew I would fall and the rest of us.

Jesus, being known as the last Adam in 1 Corinthians 15:45, shows believers how to stand on God's Word. It states "The first man was named Adam, and the Scriptures tell us that he was a living person. But Jesus, who may be called the last Adam, is a life-giving spirit." The blueprint that Jesus left us can also be found in Psalm 1:3. We must apply that same truth to our lives. It says,

"And he shall be like a tree planted by the rivers of living water, that bringeth forth his fruit in his season; his leaf shall not wither; and whatsoever he doeth shall prosper."

The third tactic and most strategic plan of the Enemy is that he alters God's Word to lure us into sin. It would be ignorant of me to not understand how the Enemy works. I needed to become more aware of his maneuvers and how he operates.

In the garden, the serpent knew exactly what the Lord had told Adam and Eve regarding the tree of life. When he approached Eve in Genesis 3:2, she too understood clearly what God had said. She states, *"We may eat the fruit of the trees in the garden: but of the fruit of the tree, which is in the midst of the garden, God said, 'You shall not eat it, nor shall you touch it, lest you die.'"*

So here is the glitch that the serpent uses in verse 4: "Then the serpent said to the woman, *'You will not surely die. For God knows that on the day you eat of it your eyes will be opened, and you will be like God, knowing good and evil.'"*

Again, the Enemy capitalizes on Eve's weakness through manipulation. He twists the Word of God by telling Eve she would not die. But what He omitted was God's intention in what He said to Adam and Eve. God's initial plan when He created mankind was to dwell among them forever with no separation. Adam and Eve were holy before God. The Lord's presence was with them. When the Lord said that if they eat, they will surely die, He meant that their lives would have an expiration date and they would return to the dust from which they came. If Adam and Eve had obeyed God, there would be no death. They would have lived forever with the Lord.

In the garden, they were pure and sanctified. The serpent used the spirit of pride by telling Eve that they would be like God, knowing good and evil. Genesis 3:6-7 says, *"The woman stared at the fruit. It looked beautiful and tasty. She wanted the wisdom that it would give her, and she ate some of the fruit. Her husband was with her, so she gave some to him, and he ate too."*

Satan learned the hard way that there could be only one God in heaven and earth. Jesus references this account in Luke 10:18 when He says, *"I saw Satan fall like lightning from heaven."* He continues in verse 19: *"I have given you authority to trample on snakes and scorpions and to overcome all the power of the enemy; nothing will harm you."*

As I sat in reflection, I began to praise God for Jesus because He came as the second Adam to redeem us. He came to right my wrong plus those that occurred in the garden.

The fourth and final tactic of the serpent in the garden is that he set Adam and Eve up to fail. Today, more than ever, Satan approaches us under the guise of being our helper. He pretends to be our friend. But we must know we have one helper, and one true friend who whispers what we should and shouldn't do. He is the Holy Spirit. But Satan, being a serial copycat, always masks himself to seem good, as if he's looking out for our best interest.

If you are like me, you found out the hard way that Satan being "good" is farthest from the truth. As mentioned before, Satan knew very well that God had commanded Adam and Eve to refrain from eating from the tree of the knowledge of good and evil. Satan also knows from his own encounters with the Lord, that God's Word stands. I'm very sure that it hurt the heart of God that He had to enforce judgment on His first offspring.

But God, being a perfect Father, had to discipline and reinforce His Word with His children. When the Lord cast out Adam and Eve from Eden, it was a consequence of their disobedience.

A good parent always corrects. Wise correction is done through love. A good parent would not observe their child going in the wrong way without rebuking him. A good parent would not just sit on the sidelines and allow their child to be deceived or bullied either.

I believe there is an internal sixth sense or intuition that mothers and fathers receive when they become parents. As a child, my mom could tell when I had done something sneaky or wrong without being physically present when I did it. The same with my dad. He could discern and speak into me whenever I felt confused, frustrated, or stuck throughout different phases of my life.

In various situations, my mom and dad would be the voice of reason for each other. At times, one of them just couldn't understand me but the other did. As parents working together, they tried as best they could to be good parents, not perfect, but doing their best.

Likewise, as children, our convictions can cause us to avoid those closest to us. Therefore, because of the guilt and shame we feel, we internalize our failures. Specifically, those we feel were most disappointing.

A good parent knows when you've gone off course. Genesis 3:7 says, *"At once they saw what they had done, and they realized they were naked. Then they sewed fig leaves together to cover themselves."*

As children, our fathers are our protective covering until we marry. In our parents' house, we must obey the rules and abide by what they say. If you don't obey, then you must face and deal with the consequences of your actions. In the garden, God was Adam and Eve's protective covering. Yet once they stepped outside the will of God, they were exposed. Their eyes were indeed opened, but it was in a way God did not intend. Genesis 3:8 recounts how Adam and Eve responded to God their Father after their sin.

"Late in the afternoon, when the breeze began to blow, the man and the woman heard the Lord God walking in the garden,

so they hid behind some trees." Their eyes were opened to guilt and shame.

God never intended us to live that way. That is a ploy of the Enemy. God wants us to live in freedom and holiness with Him. Satan always operates opposite of God. His intention is to get God's children to defy Him. Satan knows disobedience to God is a sin. He also knows that once we open the door to sin in our lives, it separates us from a perfect and holy God.

The serpent did all he could to make it look as if God had failed. He tried to paint the picture of God being unfit as a Father who created children who could not obey Him. He wanted to, in a sense, "show God up" and discount Him for giving authority to man instead of him.

It was foolish of them to think they could hide from the Creator of the universe. Just like it was foolish of me to think I could hide from God when I sinned. But that's one of the fruits of sin. It condemns us. Sin makes us feel disgraced and shameful. God did not create us to partake in sin but in His great love for us, He has given us free will.

In my home, there was love, but there was also discipline. Although we may have gotten away with more than we'd like to admit, my siblings and I grew up knowing that there would be consequences for our actions—especially if we acted out of character. We were verbally reprimanded and/or sent to our room.

Sometimes when our actions did not require words to be spoken, we were corrected with my parent's personal assistant: the belt. In most ethnic cultures, if you are of age and refuse to listen or go too far, parents typically force you to change your address and kick you out.

Genesis 3:23-24 describes what happened like this: *"Therefore the Lord God sent him out of the garden of Eden to till the ground from which he was taken. So He drove out the man; and He placed cherubim at the east of the garden of Eden, and a flaming sword which turned every way, to guard the way to the tree of life."*

In Genesis 3:11, we see God's confrontation and judgment of all three participants. Although this situation was unfortunate, the curse of man was administered. Genesis 3:11-13 gives an in-depth look at the conversation that took place between God, Adam, Eve, and the serpent.

I found it quite interesting that when God questioned Adam about what happened, he immediately blamed Eve and even God! We see it in Genesis 3:12 when Adam responds, *"The woman whom You gave to be with me, she gave me of the tree, and I ate."* Next, in verse 13, the Lord questions Eve and she responds, *"The serpent deceived me, and I ate."* Finally, the Lord confronts the serpent and then He brings judgment without asking him anything. The Lord says:

"Because you have done this, you are cursed more than all cattle, and more than every beast of the field. On your belly you shall go, and you shall eat dust all the days of your life. I will put enmity between you and the woman, and between your seed and her Seed; He shall bruise your head, and you shall bruise His heel."

(Genesis 3:14-15)

I sat and had a lot of questions after reading this text. I had read it many times before, but this time, the Lord granted me deeper spiritual discernment. I could see the whole picture with new eyes. The first thing I noticed is that God questioned Adam first. "Why not Eve or the serpent?" I asked. Then God in all His mercy answered me and said,

I am a God of order. I created Adam first for a reason. I gave my commands and directives to him first. My directives were to be obeyed and enforced by Adam. I am His protective covering. Anytime he steps outside of My will, he steps outside of My covering. I gave him authority over all things I created. I gave him position and power. I created Adam to be a visionary. He was called to see beyond the natural. He is to be alert and aware. I called Adam to be accountable. Not only for his actions, but for all those I gave him responsibility over.

The Lord continued and said, *"Adam took his eyes off Me. Even in a split second, it was enough to make him fall. Yes, I gave him the woman. I birthed her from a man. I created her to be his helper. They were made to walk together in unity and not separate from each other. The two became one."*

As I processed all the questions in my head, the Lord posed a few questions to me. He asked, *"How did Eve get separated from man long enough to be deceived? How was the serpent able to converse with her so long without a disruption or an objection from Adam? I will tell you why."* He said, *"His eyes were removed from Me. Remember, I made them perfect. They were in communion with Me. My Spirit was one with them. The only way to disconnect from Me is if your eyes are turned away from Me and fixated on something else. That opens the door to distractions."*

The Lord heard my thoughts and answered me aloud. He said,

> *Adam took his own eyes off Me. His focus was away from Me. He allowed the woman to distract and influence him. Adam, without even realizing it, fixed his eyes on himself, his wife, and the tangible and physical blessings I had given him. He abandoned and aborted*

his Spirit-man. The Spirit is the part of man that is divinely connected to Me.

Had he been spiritually inclined, he would have heard Me speaking when I asked him, 'Where is your wife?' He would've heard Me when I said to be her protective covering. He would have heard Me when I warned him there was a serpent in the garden who wanted to deceive him. Adam's spiritual ears were not in tune with Me. He was spiritually deaf and blinded by distractions. Adam put his confidence in the gift I gave him through the woman, and he forgot to acknowledge the giver of the gift. He couldn't hear or see. Therefore, the serpent had access to them once their eyes were off Me.

I was flabbergasted at the Lord's retort. His response was insightful. Without delay, I reflected on the cliché, "The eyes are the windows to the soul." Evidently, there is some truth to that, and the Enemy used it to his advantage. I paused for a moment in awe of this revelation. We don't read this account in the Bible, but I know it was breathed by the Holy Spirit! I felt like I was interviewing the Father.

It was as if He was being reflective. It felt as though the sequence of events that occurred in the beginning of time had just happened. Events that turned the world upside down. There I was, getting these accounts from the One who had a front-row seat at it all. He was and is the all-knowing and all-seeing God. I finally got it. Hearing it from the Creator's perspective made more sense.

Adam had gotten out of position, out of order. I gave him his wife. Before I created her, I gave him commands and instructions to follow. Adam was given his purpose and identity. I expected him to carry out my commands and uphold them because I gave them to him first. I am a God of order.

I knew this to be true because in Genesis 3:11, the Lord asks Adam, *"Have you eaten from the tree of which I commanded you that you should not eat?"* God questioned Adam first, not Eve because Adam was given authority over the garden and his wife. He was made to be her protector, spiritual covering, and his responsibility.

I processed all the Lord had said. Instantaneously, my mind pondered on Eve. "What happened to her?" I asked. The Lord chuckled at me saying, *"I knew you would ask that. Eve was created to be a suitable companion for Adam. She was made a little weaker than him, but still equal parts of Me. Eve became very zealous."*

I pondered that word in my thoughts. I remember the Lord once described me as being zealous. He interrupted my thoughts and responded ever so reassuringly.

"It isn't zeal that is bad daughter;
it is zeal without knowledge that becomes an issue."
(Proverbs 19:2)

He continued,

Eve desired things like unto Adam but that was not how she was made to function. She was made to submit to him as her protective covering. When she evaded that covering, she evaded her protection. Again, out of order. A house divided will crumble and fall, my daughter (Matthew 12:25). *Can two walk together unless agreed?* (Amos 3:3)

There He was, the living Word quoting His very words found in Scripture. It made me realize just how powerful the Word of God is. He is faithful to His written Word and that floored me!

My last and final observation was that the Lord asked

Adam and Eve what they had done, not the serpent. His answer was one word filled with so much truth: *accountability.* God hit the nail on the head!

He continued saying,

I wanted them to be accountable for their actions. When I ask a question, it doesn't mean that I don't already know the answer. I wanted them to hold themselves responsible for their actions and that didn't happen. Adam placed blame on Me, then Eve. Eve placed blamed on the serpent. I didn't have to ask the serpent why because he has already shown himself to Me. I am not surprised by his actions or the actions of My offspring. What I desire from all My children are contrite hearts and broken spirits when they fall and make bad decisions. 'The Lord is near to those who have a broken heart and have a contrite spirit' (Psalm 34:18).

They did not submit themselves and admit their wrong. I asked them both a question but instead of answering and repenting, in pride, they failed to take responsibility for their own failures and disobedience.

What the Enemy didn't know is that God already had a

plan in place to redeem us to righteousness through Jesus. In Romans 2:11-13, Paul explains it perfectly when he states:

For God does not show favoritism. All who sin apart from the law will also perish apart from the law, and all who sin under the law will be judged by the law. For it is not those who hear the law who are righteous in God's sight, but those who obey the law who will be declared righteous.

What many don't understand unless they receive a true revelation from God is that Eden was not a geographical place. It is not a garden that scientists can research or find fossils and remains of its existence. Eden was a dimension in the spirit-realm. When the Lord created Adam and Eve, He made them perfect and, in His image, (Psalm 139:14-18).

Satan was and has always been jealous of the relationship between God and His children. God has given man free will and rule over every creation in the earth. He has filled them with His Spirit and the breath of life rotates in and out our nostrils. Through Jesus, we are co-heirs in the kingdom of heaven. Satan wanted God's throne and all the glory for himself. Thus, he attempted to carry out anarchy in heaven as an angel of light.

CHAPTER 19

᠕

Sowing and Reaping

"Don't be misled—you cannot mock the justice of God.
You will always harvest what you plant."
(Galatians 6:7, NLT)

O ur choices can either have good or bad outcomes. I
love David's approach to God after he quickly
learned his sins could not simply be covered up from the
Lord. He grasps that truth in Psalm 139:7; *"Where can I go*
from Your Spirit? Or where can I flee from Your presence? If I
ascend into heaven, You are there; If I make my bed in hell, behold,
You are there."

Verse 15 states, *"My frame was not hidden from you when I*
was made in the secret place, when I was woven together in the
depths of the earth. Your eyes saw my unformed body; all the days
ordained for me were written in Your book before any of them came
to be."

When King David first sinned before God, he too

thought that he could cover it up. In 2 Samuel 12:14-27, David had Bathsheba's husband Uriah killed after committing adultery with her. God then sent the prophet Nathan to expose his sin and to bring judgment upon him. The prophet Nathan told David God would strike his firstborn son. David humbled himself before the Lord and accepted His correction. Later, through David's love, devotion, holy fear, and adoration of the Lord, God honored David and made a covenant with him. *"I have made a covenant with My chosen, I have sworn to My servant David: "Your seed I will establish forever and build up your throne to all generations."* (Psalm 89:3)

I couldn't help but think of how gracious and merciful the Lord was to David. He had committed many sins. Yet, God still forgave him and even promised his legacy would be an everlasting kingdom. The Savior, Jesus was birthed from that same lineage—the King of kings and the Lord of lords! What an honor. What an example of God's faithfulness and love.

After reading this story, I couldn't help but think about my own failures. It was almost eerie how God sent Nathan the prophet to David and how He sent Cynthia the prophet to me. I feared the Lord that day and did not want to find out what would happen had I disobeyed. That's another reason to be thankful for Jesus paying the price for the sins I committed.

The Lord always sends messages to His children to get their attention. *Are you listening or paying attention?* I was fortunate enough to get a direct message from God through His prophet that I couldn't ignore. She just happened to be my friend.

Who has God sent in your life to get your attention? What word or warning have you received but choose to reject? Are you rejecting who God is sending into your life? Is there anyone who has spoken truth into your life, but you dismissed it because of offense or pride? Take it from me, sometimes the truth hurts but I would rather hear God's truth than continue in a path that will only lead to destruction. If God is sending someone or something to get your attention, I encourage you to seek Him for yourself and take heed when He confirms. God only has good things in store for you.

The Lord was just in His judgment of me. It's not to say I got away scot-free. There were repercussions for my sins, but God's mercy is greater. Remember back when I hurt my ankle in the movie theater? Two days after that happened, I couldn't take it anymore and went to an urgent care facility. My ankle was still swollen, and I was in excruciating pain.

The prognosis was a bruised ankle, not a sprain.

Technically, a sprain is a lot worse than a bruise. However, I still suffered from pain and discomfort as if it were a sprain. It even affected my daily routine. Driving to and from work aggravated it and caused swelling from the back-and-forth manipulations between pedal and brake pads. Two years later, I still suffered from pain in my right ankle.

Last year, I prayed and prayed to God for healing. About six months after the incident, I drove myself to the E.R. I wanted to know if I had reinjured it because the pain became overbearing even while sleeping. The doctor did an X-Ray and found nothing. Then just recently, now three years later, I went to get an MRI because I was still experiencing pain from the same ankle. The MRI revealed that I had three different ligaments injured from that one incident. All this time I had been walking, dancing, and exercising with messed up ligaments. I had no idea!

As a dancer and choreographer, I was devastated. I was later sent to a specialist and the podiatrist said surgery may be necessary to correct the injury. I felt defeated and began to ponder if God had purposely turned a deaf ear to my prayers for healing. He led me to one of the Apostle Paul's writings, and I found out for myself. He led me to 2

Corinthians 12:8-10:

Three times I begged the Lord to make this suffering go away. But He replied, "My gift of undeserved grace is all you need. My power is strongest when you are weak". So, if Christ keeps giving me His power, I will gladly brag about how weak I am. Yes, I am glad to be weak or insulted or mistreated or to have troubles and sufferings if it is for Christ. Because when I am weak, I am strong.

In that moment, I surrendered. I realized and understood that although I too have been walking around with a thorn in my flesh, it was God's grace keeping me going. Three years later, I am reminded that His grace is still sufficient.

In church, I grew up just hearing about Jesus, the cross, and the resurrection. However, the fine details of this love story are what make it so beautiful. God sent Jesus to the earth on a rescue mission! It is important to understand the full extent of His suffering, sacrifice, and the salvation He offers us. It's amazing!

The penalty for my mistakes and misfortunes was death. Thankfully, instead of paying the price of justice, the merciful God sent someone in our place. This truth created a deeper sense of appreciation for the sacrifice of Jesus

Christ. At last, I could experience the love He poured out for me. The love of Jesus permeated into my soul. I saw God and Jesus in a new light. They were no longer separate entities in my eyes. The Father and the Son complemented and completed each other. In my eyes, they are one and the same.

Jesus descended to the earth to build a bridge. That bridge would reestablish heaven on the earth. Jesus came to extend a second invitation to be in the presence of God on earth again as He intended through His blood! Our acceptance of Him as our Savior means we will once again live forever with God! I am so grateful He never had a plan B. His plan A was and still is to spend eternity with us, His children. I shouted when I got a deeper revelation of that truth.

CHAPTER 20

The Fruit of the Spirit; the Healing Garden

"But the fruit of the Spirit is love, joy, peace, forbearance,
kindness, goodness, faithfulness."
(Galatians 5:22, NIV)

T he parental characteristics of God activated my curiosity in the totality of who He is. I learned that there were both fraternal and maternal facets of Him. He was strong and protective when I needed to be rescued, and on the other side, He was nurturing and reassuring when I just longed to know I was loved and understood.

My regard for Jesus took a pivotal shift. He became the love I had been searching for my entire life! It was weird at first, but as I thought of all my failed relationships and the men who had hurt me, Jesus stood out as the man of my dreams. He loved me unconditionally.

Jesus died for me literally, not figuratively speaking. He

came to fix me from my brokenness. He came to heal my broken heart. He came to snatch me up to spend forever with me. No man I encountered on this earth offered me that. All Jesus wanted in return was my love above any and everything. How is that an even exchange? He risked and gave up much more than I could ever imagine! He did it just for me.

To fully embrace God's love and acceptance of me, I had to revisit pivotal periods in my life. God figuratively took me back to "The Shack," which is one of my favorite movies. I needed to confront previous soul ties and agreements made with the Enemy unbeknownst to me. God pinpointed the moments and instances where I had taken my eyes off Him. He showed me ways that I put my trust in man instead of Him.

This season was lonely at times. The harsh realities of introspection were painful, hard, and difficult all at the same time. The Lord placed a huge spiritual mirror in front of me. I had no choice but to stare and confront the reflection that stared back at me. He didn't shove a mirror of condemnation in my face, but one of grace and love.

Revisiting the events that caused my heart to self-protect was like a real-life "Back to the Future" experience for me. It also reminded me of the story of Scrooge, a bitter old man who gets a visit from the ghost of Christmas past, present, and future.

The ghost gives strategic presentations of the main character's (Scrooge) life. The details of his past and present dictate the outcome of his future if he doesn't make necessary changes in his heart and how he relates to others. Isn't that just like the Holy Spirit? He is that real-life (Holy) Ghost that Jesus sent to help us in our time of need.

In this season of my life, God began to reveal areas where my heart needed a spiritual transplant. As I drew closer to Him, self-righteousness began to grow an ego. Everybody's Christian walk needed to be pointed out in my eyes. I became the judge internally. It became so easy for me to point out my neighbor's flaws. I started to give unsolicited advice to others as I felt necessary. The Lord exposed a harsh reality in me. I become insensitive to the personal journey of others.

My crosswalk overshadowed where others were now. I was super judgmental and critical of people without even knowing it. Countless times, God positioned me to minister to friends, co-workers, or even family members, but I missed the mark.

Bitterness and past hurts rushed in like a flood as God showed me that I had layers of unforgiveness and resentment. I got a high from pointing out other people's weaknesses and failures. I swiftly forgot that once upon a time, the same shortcomings were my own. This is the root of self-righteousness. God specializes in doing the impossible. But somehow, I had fallen into the trap that many other Christians tend to slip into unbeknownst to them.

The gift of salvation and the amazing transformation we experience has little to do with us and more to do with Jesus and the work of the cross. God, being the thorough Father He is, gave me a crash course on something He specializes in and that is *grace*. It is a word I had heard often, but honestly, I never understood how to extend it. Grace is something I pleaded with the Lord for whenever I had fallen short. However, it is something I failed to extend to others.

My tolerance level was short with others who didn't agree with me. If someone rubbed me the wrong way or offended me, I had a Christian right to throw the devil card at them. If someone close to me called me out or was brutally honest about my character flaws, I punished them by being passive-aggressive and silent.

The Lord's spiritual mirror was beginning to mimic my bathroom mirror whenever I took a hot shower. My mirror was so filled with spiritual hindrances under the guise of steam that it clouded my reflection. I could no longer see myself in others. That type of logic was dangerous to my witness.

The Lord taught me that my self-proclaimed perfectionism was not a good character trait to brag about. Sure, it sounds good to the world when we deem ourselves as "perfectionists" in our work ethic. However, the Holy Spirit translates this type of thinking as no different from eating the forbidden fruit. Why? Because it's rooted in pride and control. What we are really conveying to the world is our own narcissism.

I wondered why the Lord was taking me through this process. Saving my spirit and soul from the Enemy's grasp wasn't enough. Now, He had to do spiritual surgery from the inside out. I love that about my Father. He cares deeply about the total person. That includes the mind, body, soul, and spirit.

The next phase of healing the Lord took me through was my past relationships. Not just James but all of them. The Lord began to show me where the different layers of pain, mistrust, and bitterness stemmed from. He took me back into my past to see how the areas of pain and rejection had impacted me.

Every relationship I had been in was first and foremost an unauthorized relationship. Yes, I had prayed to God for direction, but I didn't heed the warning signs. For one, none of my ex-boyfriends had a serious relationship with Jesus. Some of them went to church, but their spiritual foundation was inadequate for where God was taking me.

I desired a man who was mature and inclined to the voice of God. I wanted someone who was a spiritual leader in his public and private life. While pondering the thought, I realized that I had spent fifty percent of my time trying to lead these men to Christ. Deep down inside, I knew that I didn't want a man who was a babe in Christ. I wanted and needed a seasoned veteran.

I desired a man of prayer, fasting, studying, and applying the Word of God. I wanted someone who could lead, and I would willingly follow. I wanted someone who loved me for me and treated me with respect—flaws and all—not who they were trying to make me be.

I knew all of this, yet I did what many women end up doing. I compromised. I ignored my wants and desires in a man. I compromised my faith and beliefs just to hold on to a relationship. I lowered my standards or even worse, I didn't demand them to step up to the plate out of fear of being alone. I needed to be willing to stick to my guns or let go of anyone who merely had potential. That was not my strong suit and God was showing me how much it cost me.

The end of any relationship is painful. I needed to give myself the time and space to mourn the death of each one and allow God to heal every layer of hurt. Each relationship left me with a sense of rejection and abandonment. The Lord revealed to me areas where I needed to release forgiveness to those individuals who had hurt me. It wasn't until the Great Physician did a spiritual x-ray of my heart, that I finally realized how much pain I had held on to.

This was a painful process but very necessary. I wanted to be free, and it was either the Lord's way or no way. I wanted to end the insanity of doing relationships the same way and expecting different results. Change had to begin with me. I was thankful that the Father loved me enough to guide me through this healing process. It was as if He was taking my hand every step of the way. When memories or circumstances got too heavy, He and His angelic host were right there to encourage me.

After each chapter of each failed relationship, I felt a door being closed. He led me to verbally release forgiveness for everything I held them accountable for. I also had to release forgiveness to myself. I had to break soul ties, mindsets, and unhealthy patterns that I had experienced in the past. This took a lot of warfare as the Enemy got busy. He wanted me to stay in spiritual bondage. I was attacked in my dreams, lost sleep, and he would even bring around the same men God was trying to deliver me from.

I was desperate to get and stay free. I quickly utilized the block option on my phone and set strict boundaries for myself. The Enemy tried many ways to trip me up. He used the ones who were the hardest to get over and sent them my way. By the help of God and the Holy Spirit, I was able to maneuver out of Satan's traps. God always gives us a way of escape if we trust Him.

The Lord then encouraged me to keep a journal so I could release what I was feeling. These journals became very therapeutic. They were filled with God's spoken word to me, answered prayers, Bible studies, testimonies, and so much more! After this season, I felt another layer fall off me and I was thankful.

The next phase of healing the Lord took me through was about my temple. *"Do you not know that your bodies are the temple of the Holy Spirit?"* (1 Corinthians 6:19)

God began to allow this truth to permeate my soul. Everything that I was allowing through my eyes, ears, mind, and mouth influenced me. Every negative connotation or thing that pulled at my heartstrings formed my thinking.

As we know, the mind is the battleground, which the Enemy uses as a strategy. He utilizes our thinking to attack us. Whatever I see, affects me, good or bad. Whatever I listen to affects me, good or bad. Whatever I think about affects me, good or bad. Therefore, Paul reminds us to think on thoughts that are true, noble, or of good report (Philippians 4:8). This means as a follower of Christ, I need to be proactive in what I allow into my spirit. I need to be aware and alert of my surroundings.

The Holy Spirit also convicted and showed me where I fell simply because of what I allowed into my soul unknowingly. It could be a movie, TV show, or reality show. The Lord pointed out how watching certain things were intoxicating my spirit. The same thing was for what or who I listened to.

I'm reminded of a parrot, talking parrots to be exact. They don't develop vocabulary on their own, they simply repeat what they hear or what they've heard. We can look at our spirits the same way. Whatever we feed the spirit internally, it will eventually produce externally. God was calling me to be accountable for what I allowed into my spirit.

He carefully revealed to me why I struggled in certain areas of my life. He showed me how some of my favorite shows or movies drew me in. My mind and imagination would ponder things I wouldn't have, had those seeds not been deposited from what I watched. It was a tactic of the Enemy to get me to lust or desire unholy things.

The Lord showed me how that song I loved so much was not just a song but a trap to keep my heart bound. The Lord's revelations in the small details of my life gave me a new appreciation for God's Word. They were no longer just a bunch of words in a sacred text. These words were life. They were living, breathing words that were activated when I applied them.

Scriptures just began to flow through my heart as I journeyed through this season of introspection with the Lord. It was like watching floating pollen in the sky during the springtime.

"The peace of God, which surpasses all understanding, will guard your hearts and minds through Christ Jesus."
(Philippians 4:7)

"Thy word have I hidden in my heart, so I won't sin against thee."
(Psalm 119:11)

"A person may think their own ways are right, but the Lord weighs the heart."
(Proverbs 21:2)

The concluding lesson the Lord wanted to teach me was how to enhance the stewardship of my body, His temple. Like millions of other people, I have two weaknesses when it comes to food: sugar and carbs. I had been battling a lot of chronic illnesses, and I heard the Lord say to me that most of them were due to my diet and lifestyle.

The Lord instructed me to do away with caffeine, sugar, and to reduce my carb intake. These simple things were subtle temptations to keep my body sick and tired. I had no energy and suffered from chronic migraines and vertigo regularly. It is still an uphill battle, but I decided to love my body.

My body is the very tool that the Lord uses to bless and reach others. If my body was sick and run down, then what good could I be to God's kingdom? Certainly, God is a healer. But again, He was calling me to be a better steward over the things He blessed me with, and I had to submit to His will.

I was motivated and set out to avoid sugar as much as possible and reduce my carb intake. I started to feel better, and the migraines decreased greatly. I am grateful to the Lord for His infinite wisdom and guidance. He was caring for me in a way I could never imagine.

The love of the Father became overwhelming. He cared

about every detail of my life. I realized then the Scripture that says He knows even the number of hairs on your head is true. He's detailed like that. The Father has a plan for me, you and all His children. He is intentional and detailed about how He prepares us for our purpose.

CHAPTER 21

❧

A Tree Planted

"Blessed is the one who does not walk in step with the wicked or stand in the way that sinners take or sit in the company of mockers, but whose delight is in the law of the Lord, and who meditates on his law, day and night. That person is like a tree planted by streams of water, which yields its fruit in season and whose leaf does not wither; whatever they do prospers."

(Psalm 1:1-4)

During this stage, the Lord led me into new territory both spiritually and physically. I started teaching at a new school after being at one school for ten years. He also transitioned me from where I worshipped and served in ministry. God started to uncover and shed light on sudden changes within my circle. I started to see slight but noticeable changes in the atmosphere. Shifts were taking place in the spiritual realm. It was apparent more so in the place of worship where I was being fed spiritually. This began to happen so frequently, that the Lord told me not to receive anything spoken over me without consulting Him first. Certain behaviors and teachings did not sit well in my soul and God did not cosign them.

Slowly but surely, I found myself being detached from the ministry where I once felt the presence of the Holy Spirit so powerfully. But in God's infinite wisdom, I realized some things I experienced and encountered that were not of Him. As my soul started to feel spiritually raped at times, I knew it was time to go, but I wouldn't make the move until the Lord said so. I can still remember to this day, one Saturday morning when the Lord woke me up. I had been in prayer, asking God for direction. I slowly drifted away and that morning, the Lord told me in a very stern and assured way, "Remove yourself!"

I swiftly obeyed. I remained in the holy fear of the Lord. His tone and command sounded like thunder. I didn't understand why all the sudden changes were taking place, but I was learning to trust God even when it didn't make sense. I realized then I know nothing, and He knows everything. There would be no arguments from me.

I began to visit churches in the neighborhood that I had not been to since I moved. I did this until the Lord directed me where He wanted me to settle.

As I prayed, I already knew where to go. I kept passing by this place near the downtown area and each time, I felt this tugging at my heart and butterflies in my belly. I would always say to the Lord, "one day." One Saturday morning, the Lord woke me up and placed this church strongly in my spirit. Recently, the church moved into another building. The Lord led me to google its new location. It was even closer to my home than the old place.

I turned on Google Maps and typed in the new address. I was astounded by what I saw. I accidentally moved up the cursor away from the church building and the camera shifted up into the sky. The sun beamed as a huge angel-shaped cloud hovered over the church. It didn't take me long to figure out where God was planting me. It was a church located right in my neighborhood.

This new transition was difficult for me. I had developed a trustworthy relationship with my brothers and sisters in Christ. The disjointing of our friendship hurt me to the core. We had gotten so close in a short period of time. I spent most of my free time with these individuals, and here I was walking away from it. My obedience to God was being tested. I had to learn that my feelings were secondary when it came to the Father's will. I saw a shift happen in the people I loved. Something just wasn't right, and God did the separating by drawing a line in the sand.

God required me to set boundaries in my relationships and friendships. He was cleaning my inner circle. The Lord highlighted specific friendships that were inequitable and one-sided. I gave more of myself than I should. I had toxic friendships that needed to end or have issues resolved. This goes back to what I allowed into my spirit.

I saw myself being influenced negatively by certain people I had been loyal to. Those friendships were draining me. No matter how many times I tried to communicate how I felt, things would go back to the same old, same old.

God was calling me to establish healthy relationships and to rid myself of anything opposite of that. Arguing, fighting, and then blaming it on the Devil was not a healthy relationship or friendship. I needed to break the cycles of inviting unhealthy relationships into my life.

I had reached a point where I had enough and even God said enough. Clear as day, the Lord commanded these words I will never forget: "You are released!" From that moment, I knew exactly what I had to do. I needed to set boundaries for myself. I could no longer hang around negativity, gossip, or toxicity. It was tainting my spirit and weighing me down. God was doing the lifting and the shifting. He had enough of me trying to please others and being in one-sided relationships.

I just couldn't take it anymore. I still genuinely love all my brothers and sisters in Christ. I will always be there for them, no doubt. But when God steps in, that's when enough is enough.

Setting boundaries became a loud anthem that the Lord was singing for me. I needed to love God and myself enough to not allow certain things, people, or circumstances to get in the way of God's purpose and plan for my life. During this transition, I cried a lot of tears. I questioned if I had heard God clearly.

My feelings tried to get the best of me, but every time that happened, God would reconfirm His Word repeatedly. I even grew angry and frustrated at times, wondering why I was alone in this process. But I soon realized that I was right in alignment with the Father's will.

This year felt like a whirlwind. God had taken me to and through things I had never imagined. This journey through my past and present was filled with many ups and downs. I shed many tears. I learned how to relinquish control over the things I really had no control over and how to be accountable for the things God blessed me with.

The Lord revealed deep and hidden pain I never recognized I had held on to. He forced me to confront the enemy within myself that was holding me back from really receiving the promises of God.

My loving Father broke my temple down to build it back up again. Still there was one more painful lesson He needed to teach me, which He saved for last.

CHAPTER 22

Deeply Rooted

"So that Christ may dwell in your hearts through faith. And I pray that you, being rooted and established in love, may have power, together with all the Lord's holy people, to grasp how wide and long and high and deep is the love of Christ, and to know this love that surpasses knowledge—that you may be filled to the measure of all the fullness of God."

(Ephesians 3:17-18)

God didn't want me to see Him as just God. He didn't want to be viewed as this distant, disconnected deity who could not understand humanity. Rather, He wanted me to see Him as my heavenly Father who cares about every detail of my life. Moreover, He wanted me to see myself the way He always saw me from the very beginning: as His daughter. But first, I needed to reconcile my issues with my earthly father.

In the beginning, I shared how my family and I had been through horrors over the past two years. Well, during that time, my dad became a person I didn't recognize. He shot verbal insults and accused my mom of things that made no sense to us. My mom would be confronted with accusations and harsh exchanges from my dad out of nowhere.

It seemed as if he made any excuse to pick a fight with her. There were times I would get a call in the middle of the night from my mom because she was awakened from her sleep by violent behavior and erratic thoughts that escaped his mind. He used words that I had never heard him say. They were hurtful and toxic. Shortly after that, I decided to move back home because I was concerned for my mother's safety and my father's health.

We sought help from church leadership, law enforcement, health specialists and doctors. The options we were given were little to none. Even reaching out to some family members didn't help. They couldn't come to terms with the things my mom told them. They didn't believe her. Of course, they were in dismay. In their minds they probably thought, *"How could this loving, kind, and patient man do the things you are saying?"* It just didn't make sense to them. So, after trying to reach out to many, my mom was left with disappointment and very little support. Her strength came from two places: God and her children.

My siblings and I were at a loss. We tried our best to support our mom and ensure her safety as much as possible. It wasn't until later that we discovered that my dad was suffering from a medical condition and a mental disorder.

He was later diagnosed with dementia/psychosis. Dementia is a broad condition of the brain that affects memory, attention, communication, reasoning, judgment and visual perception that goes beyond age-related changes in vision. Psychosis is a symptom where individuals can experience disconnect from reality. We didn't know it at the time because dad had always been a loving, caring father and husband. His symptoms just came out of nowhere.

We didn't have many options. It took me a short time to realize how many other people and families suffer this horror before they can be taken seriously and get help. My dad was getting worse. The side effects came in waves. We couldn't prepare for the unpredictable behaviors that he displayed.

I felt that as a family, we didn't get the support necessary for individuals and families dealing with this medical condition that is often times misdiagnosed as only a mental illness. My dad, mom, and our entire family all suffered in some way. My dad would get severe headaches and then his brain would send signals to his mind. These signals caused him to see, do and say things he normally wouldn't. My mother suffered verbal assaults from a stranger who had taken over her loving husband. That person was not my dad. My dad was a kind, patient, and loving man.

My siblings and I exhausted every medical and legal resource available to us. We looked for as much information and support as we could. We pleaded with professionals to find ways to get our dad the help he needed. By the same token, we were also trying to support and protect our mother emotionally and physically. It was a difficult situation to be in. My sister and I moved back home at different periods during this time. Witnessing the drastic changes in our dad's personality and seeing him struggle to try to control it was painful. Seeing our mother deal with the trauma of being the focal point of his outbursts was also difficult.

My dad loves my mom. I can remember from childhood to adulthood, my dad telling my mom "I love you" every single day. My siblings and I all witnessed his love and affection for my mom daily.

Specific laws limit how much assistance and support is available to families. In my opinion, there is insufficient support in place for medical disorders of the brain that camouflage as a mental disorder. Law enforcement, intervention specialists, and healthcare professionals should be readily available to assist those in need.

During this entire ordeal, my mother's options were extremely limited. She was told she could only call 911 and press charges if he got violent. I strongly believe that jail and prison time is not the answer for someone suffering from a medical or mental illness. How can you treat a brain or mental disorder effectively behind bars?

There must be better and effective laws passed to support and assist families who have and are currently going through this. Also, what about the spouses and families who must deal with the trauma during and even after the storm? I know that there is so much therapy and counseling available now, but at that time, we were not offered many solutions.

My mom suffered the most through this. She has been the rock for our family. Her inner strength, giving spirit and faith in the Lord during this whole ordeal rooted me in my faith. She has inspired our family with her tenacity, grace and willingness to forgive. She honored her vows: "For better or worse, through sickness and health."

My dad was always healthy and never once spent a night in the hospital. He eventually received counseling from a psychotherapist, medication, and assistance from intervention specialists. It has been a long and winding road. By the grace of God, my father hasn't had any more episodes like he had in the past. Also, he and my mom are still together and have just celebrated their 40th wedding anniversary.

I noticed that there was residue in my heart, mind, and soul during this chapter of my life. During this storm, I was in survival mode. I did all that I knew to do to provide spiritual, emotional, and physical support to my parents. In retrospect, I was burning on fumes. I did what I had to do to survive. My main concern was my parents and making sure they were both safe. Then as the storm passed, the internal effects of my dad's illness began to weigh heavily on me.

As I settled into my new place, I felt anger, resentment, and disappointment toward God and my dad. I asked myself unreasonable questions but received no answers. Why couldn't my dad resist the urge to react the way his brain was telling him to? How come he wasn't spiritually strong enough to combat this attack against his mind? How could he not see how much his actions were hurting our family? Why couldn't he stop? As the questions flew into my mind, tears flooded my eyes.

I lost trust in the man I had always looked to for love and assurance. I felt betrayed by the man who taught me the Word of God and how a man should treat a woman. My view of my father and men in general became distorted. I had trust issues. I lost faith in God because I couldn't understand why He allowed all of this to happen. I prayed and cried until I couldn't anymore.

When my dad started to get better, little by little, I saw our prayers being answered. They weren't answered in the way I thought or expected, but God was faithful through all of it.

The Lord began to show me the ways He was there with me and my family. He showed me how His mercy and grace were present even when we lost hope. There were seasons where the effects of dad's illness began to affect not just me, but our entire family. The Enemy came in and tried to bring confusion and division between us. Through every tear and frustration, God was there gluing back the pieces of my shattered heart. Some days, I felt as if I was in the lion's den. My character was questioned, and I was emotionally drained. The spirit of accusation and dissension tried its best to knock me down; but still, God remained faithful and my spirit was still intact.

There were moments when God and I had necessary and honest conversations. I held on to a lot of pain and it was eating me up inside.

The Lord was calling me to be healed from the inside out. This was the first phase: confronting what I identified with. I had to put the Devil in his place by standing up for myself. I no longer sat idle as the accuser tried to drag my name in the mud. I fought with God's Word and the power of love. Forgiveness, extending grace, and loving mercy became pillars for me on this new journey.

I recognized how imperative it is to release forgiveness to those who wrong you. The Lord taught me that releasing forgiveness is just as important as asking for forgiveness. True forgiveness is when you can forgive with or without an apology. The Lord tore down another layer of me, but I knew He wasn't done yet. God had an even larger battle waiting for me to fight. I needed to deal with my daddy issues.

The way I regarded my dad changed. What happened to him not only affected our relationship, but it also tainted my relationship with the Lord. For one, I didn't see God as my Father. I perceived and encountered Him as God but not my Father. I couldn't come to terms with why this happened to our family. It seemed as if we lived in a shielded cocoon of some sort. Sure, we had our ups and downs, but nothing to this extent.

I was living in a bubble when it came to my family. We had always been so close and loving. My immediate family had never been through trauma like this. It caught us completely off guard. We never faced a problem too difficult to overcome with the Lord's help. This time, I felt the Lord's silence and the man I leaned on for spiritual guidance was going through spiritual and mental turmoil.

The Lord started to reveal to me that I needed to forgive my father. He showed me how I secretly held bitterness and resentment in my heart toward him and that I needed to be healed from that. I felt like the little daddy's girl in me needed an explanation to why her hero couldn't save the day. Why wasn't he strong enough to fight this?

Soon, my investigation and research of dementia and mental illnesses shed more light on the situation for me. His brain was impaired, and he couldn't control his actions. To someone on the outside, it looked like he was intentionally being hurtful with no self-control. The truth is, he was fighting it as much as he could. We just couldn't see his silent struggles. I became more empathetic to what my dad was going through and tried to educate myself as much as possible, so I would know what to expect from anyone who suffered from dementia.

Soon, my dad and I sat down and had a candid talk about his ordeal. I released and expressed to him my silent pain and struggles. My dad listened and then shared with me his private battles and how he fought against them. Then, something unexpected happened. My dad apologized to me for the trauma I had dealt with and asked for my forgiveness. By this time, he had apologized profusely to my mom and the rest of the family for everything we went through. Not that he needed to, but once he did, I felt a sheet of pain slide off my heart. It was like in that moment, God erased every pain that I felt. That was the man I had grown to know and love. My dad has a very humble spirit. Being angry and aggressive is out of character for him. He recalled to me one day when God revealed to him how even the Enemy capitalized on his illness.

My dad told me how he repented to the Lord for allowing the Enemy to do so. I stopped him right there. I could not sit there and allow him to take the blame for his illness. Yes, he did things that affected us, but he had no control over them. When he shared with me how the Enemy manipulated and capitalized on his weakness, I was not surprised. When I thought about how Jesus healed many people from demonic possession, it wasn't so farfetched. When I looked with spiritual and not scientific eyes, what my father told me began to make sense.

I realized that many mental illnesses would be categorized under demonic possession if we were living in the time of Jesus. It is truly evident based on the behaviors that were exhibited from people who were possessed by demons. They displayed behaviors such as violence, aggression, cutting themselves, compulsions, seeing things that aren't real, etc. I am not discounting the medical factors or diagnoses, but I am familiar with the enemy and how he uses our weaknesses to destroy us.

That truth looked, smelled, and sounded like him. Satan wanted to destroy my dad and our entire family. Thankfully, with much prayer, warfare, and help from the doctors, my dad has been delivered from psychosis.

With the Lord's help, I was able to forgive and release my dad from blame. We became father and daughter again. He is back to his happy, joyful ways, and I am so grateful to God. He is once again the family jokester. Most importantly, he has learned to put his trust in the (Almighty God) as he would say, even more.

CHAPTER 23

❧

In Spirit and in Truth

"But the time is coming and, it is here! When True Worshippers will worship in spirit and truth. The Father looks for those who worship Him in this way. God is Spirit, and it is necessary to worship God in spirit and truth."

(John 4:23-24)

The next phase for me was reestablishing my relationship with the Lord. By this time, I had been attending another church near my home. The people there seemed warm and welcoming, but I couldn't help but feel alone. I didn't know anyone there. My only reason for attending was because I felt God leading me. I just wasn't sure why.

The pastor seemed down to earth. He preached the gospel in a simplistic way. There was nothing grand or showy about his demeanor. He dressed casually and so did everyone else. It was comforting to sit and receive the Word without any expectations placed on me.

I was the worship leader where I previously served. Every week I felt the pressure of wanting to make sure worship went smoothly and I was prepared to minister. I took my job seriously. Leading people into the presence of God was not something I took lightly. I examined myself and went before the Lord to ensure I was prepared both spiritually and mentally.

Cynthia had felt the Lord leading her away from our previous ministry as well. I knew it was confirmation that I wasn't alone in what I felt the Lord leading me to do when I left.

One day, Cynthia invited me to hear a gospel artist sing. His name is Anthony Evans Jr. She was attending this church called CBG (Church by the Glades) and said he was there regularly. I didn't know who he was. She told me he was Dr. Tony Evans' son. Of course, I knew of Tony Evans because my dad has been a fan of his since I was a kid. I remember listening to Dr. Evans' tapes with my dad and seeing most of his books on my dad's bookshelf. Dad's study was filled with devotionals and books from Dr. Evans. They especially came out whenever my dad prepared for a sermon. Even still, every time Cynthia invited me to Church by the Glades, I'd find some lame excuse not to go.

But then, something changed. It is a Sunday I will never

forget. I call this day "beauty for ashes." It was June 23, 2019. Cynthia told me that Anthony Evans Jr. was in town again and invited me to go to church with her that evening. I said I'd think about it because I ran out of excuses.

That day, I went from zero to sixty within minutes. I went to my church that morning praising God with all my might. But then, my praise turned into pain right after service. I was heartbroken by a situation that afternoon. It was yet another attack from the enemy. He is always doing the most whenever I am happy or in alignment with the Lord. It literally came out of nowhere. I was so overcome by emotion. My flesh just wanted to stay home and cry. In fact, that's exactly what I did. I cried out to the Lord feeling defeated and mentally drained. Of course, my friend Cynthia wasn't having any of it. She showed up at my door after she called to see if I was ready. She heard the crack in my voice and knew it was time for some spiritual intervention. Cynthia prayed and beckoned the Lord to comfort and give me peace. Then, she threatened to drag me out if I didn't go with her to CBG. I didn't want to, but I knew how persistent she was, so I went.

Once we arrived, I felt like I was walking into a concert. There was this huge stage, bright LED lights, and about two thousand seats.

Is this a church? I thought. I looked over at Cynthia as she read my face. I felt overwhelmed. The church looked beautiful, but I had never seen anything like it! People were drinking coffee they had bought from the coffee shop in the lobby. I was old school; I wasn't used to this way of doing church. The service started, and the lights nearly blinded me.

Next, Anthony Evans came out and the crowd went wild. He had a bald head and a body like a running back. When he opened his mouth to sing, I was stunned. This huge, powerhouse voice bellowed from his mouth. He was visiting to lead worship, and I was intrigued. I wasn't attracted to him or anything, but I didn't expect all that to come out of his mouth. His voice was powerful.

As Anthony Evans sang the last song of his set, the sad and defeated emotions left me. I was careful not to allow the lights and the stage to affect me. But then I asked myself, why not? Why shouldn't Jesus get all the lights and glamour? Isn't He more worthy than the celebrities that we admire? Beyond that, they don't know us, and they didn't die for us. But Jesus did.

My perspective changed in an instant. I prejudged the motives of the worship leaders on stage with Anthony Evans. For a minute, I even questioned Anthony. I wondered if it was real for him or if gospel music was his plan B if he didn't make it in the secular world. I know my thinking was harsh, but you would be surprised how many worship leaders and gospel artists have fallen victim to stealing God's glory. It's not awfully hard to. I knew it because I had been there myself. The Enemy slithers his way into the minds of many who were created to lead others to God in worship.

Remember Lucifer was the leader of praise and worship in heaven. It was his desire to receive the glory that only belongs to God in heaven. He disguises himself as an angel of light, beautiful to look at. He received promotion from God to lead the angelic host in worship to God and what did he do? He took his eyes off God his Creator and put them on himself.

Lucifer was convincing enough to persuade many other angels to follow suit. But God wasn't having it. There is one God. So, God kicked Lucifer out of heaven along with the other angels who succumbed to his evil tactics. They are called the fallen angels. The worst part of it is that unlike us, they cannot repent to God and get a second chance. They have already been sentenced and condemned along with Lucifer.

This truth makes me even more thankful and grateful for the love and the mercies of God. I thought about the many times I had unknowingly placed an idol before God or even esteemed myself more than I should. However, each scenario came with correction. I learned quickly how dangerous it could be to even taste the slightest piece of God's glory.

That same pride and vanity caused Adam and Eve to be deceived by the serpent. They wanted to obtain a level of knowledge meant only for God. It was wisdom that wasn't theirs to obtain. Because of this, our spirits are in a constant battle with our human nature. Ego and pride want to do things their way. They want recognition and to be praised by others. Pride can cause us to slip into a deep dark slope of deception if we are not careful.

As Anthony Evans wrapped up his set, I purchased his CD entitled "Altared." Amazingly, that's exactly how I felt after an hour-and-a-half of listening to him lead the congregants of Church by the Glades in worship.

I felt passion in his voice as he sang to the Lord. Although his voice was already beast mode, there was a sense of vulnerability in it as well. Anthony's voice carried a sound that felt like it was personally composed by the Lord. It's hard to put into words. But it's something that only a fellow worship leader could hear with spiritual ears. Anthony's songs of worship sounded like an unapologetic cry out unto the Lord. A cry that was loud enough to wake me up.

I appreciated that from him. My prejudgment of him quickly diminished after I felt a special anointing in his voice. It came over me subtly, but his ministry in song was like a weight being lifted off my shoulders. That heavy burden that I came in with, was gone. A sense of joy and peace was in his music. I found hope and strength again.

Before service was over, one of the pastors came out to dismiss us. He announced that Anthony would have his new CD "Altared" available for any donation amount. I thought that was divine and dope, so I hopped in line right after service to purchase it.

Cynthia and I met up in the lobby to get tea and we headed out. I didn't wait until I arrived home to listen to Anthony Evans' CD. I opened that bad boy with my keys and popped it in Cynthia's player.

We turned up the music in the car and worshipped all the way home. Something had been altered in me. I realized how much I missed this feeling. I felt a freedom rise in me as I played each song when I got home. Suddenly, I realized that I missed being what I knew I was called to be, a worship leader.

I started to seek the Lord's face about the matter. I led worship every day in my home, but I missed the fellowship of other believers in worship. I missed using my voice for

God's glory. As I prayed, I looked online to see the areas in ministry where I could serve at the church I was currently attending. I scrolled through them and saw a link for the worship ministry. I immediately clicked the button to get more info and found out that auditions were held to be on the worship team. I scheduled an appointment to meet with the worship leader at my campus and the rest is history.

After auditioning, I made the team, and I was elated the Lord had answered another prayer of mine. Being a pew member was never my forte. I needed to be involved in ministry. I owed God my life and I wanted to use each gift He placed in me for His glory.

This season of coming out of retirement from singing was rewarding but did not happen without some hurdles. I had never had vocal lessons or had professional training as a singer. Singing was something that came naturally for me since I was five years old. I grew up singing and mimicking songs by Whitney Houston, Mariah Carey, and Toni Braxton.

As a child and into my young adulthood, I had always sung in the choir or the praise team. I quickly learned that things were a bit different from what I was used to at the church I was serving in. For me, it felt mechanical. A system and app were used to prepare for worship. I was used to depending on the Holy Spirit and allowing Him to lead me in worship. I knew He resided in me there but felt a lack of invitation to include Him in our worship.

I found myself struggling with things I couldn't control. For me, it was hard to submit and trust. In the previous ministry I served in, I was humiliated in front of others when I couldn't sing a note or song the way it was expected of me. While leading worship, I found myself being annoyed with last-minute changes or how certain things were being done. Little did I know that God was highlighting my issues with trust and submission to authority.

Every time I was corrected or received constructive criticism; it struck a nerve. I passively contained it, but I knew that eventually, I would explode if I didn't address or confront it.

I prayed about it to the Lord. It was then that He began to reveal the tactics of the Enemy. He showed me how the Devil tried to bring confusion on our team. The Lord also revealed more layers of me that needed to be peeled away.

One day, out of nowhere, the Lord showed me a vision that pinpointed the exact moment when I lost trust and confidence in my ability to sing. He showed me an image of myself in tears in a bathroom crying after I had been spiritually raped by a leader during a conference. I was verbally humiliated and felt demeaned in front of others by those who were considered "anointed".

The image was so painful that I burst into tears all over again like it had just happened. I knew that the Lord was not trying to hurt me, but that He wanted to heal me from all the traumas of my past. It was then and there that I realized I had been fighting against progression and God developing me as a worship leader.

I needed to discern when the correction I received was beneficial for me and when it was my flesh getting in the way. The Lord had placed individuals in my life to grow and develop me for His glory. I didn't want to get in the way of that any longer. So, I swallowed my pride and reflected on a message that the Lord had given me earlier in that season. "Submit to God, (and everyone I have given to shepherd you). Resist the Devil, and he will flee." That stayed with me every time I found myself being challenged or pushed. In the long run, it was for my good.

Sometimes the lessons God wants to teach us are painful, frustrating, and difficult. The Enemy will even attempt to make you think it's too hard or not worth the stress. But I learned a long time ago that his goal is to get me to quit. God is a good Father. He doesn't always give us what makes us comfortable but what's best for us.

In the long run, I learned how to actively protect and exercise my vocal cords. Over the years, I had never been intentional about caring or nurturing my voice. I hadn't grasped the concept that my voice is a musical instrument. My vocal cords were just as important as the keyboard, guitar, and the drums. They were all created for the glory of God, and we must be good stewards of them.

I wanted to grow up in God. I desired the humility and submission of Jesus to be an example I followed and not just an idea. I learned to willingly submit to my spiritual leaders. Submission didn't mean that I agreed with everything they did or said. I went to God to fight the necessary battles whenever I felt unjustly treated or misunderstood. Submission activated God to move on my behalf even more because I was in obedience to Him, not just man.

I started to feel a shift in my spirit. There was something in my belly that needed to be birthed. The only problem was that I didn't know what it was. I began to study and search the Scriptures more. The Lord was inviting me to go back to the basics in His written Word. I found so much truth and revelation from Scriptures that I often breezed through due to familiarity. But the living Word, Jesus, was calling me higher.

I felt this urge to go deeper in God. I wanted to know the

character of Jesus beyond quotations. I wanted the words that He spoke over me to come alive in my life. The Lord took me back even before the Garden of Eden. He took me to when the earth was without form.

CHAPTER 24

✥

The Ruah-Breath of God

"Then the Lord God formed the man of dust from the ground and
breathed into his nostrils the breath of life,
and the man became a living creature."

(Genesis 2:7)

T he Father took me beyond the beginning when there
was darkness and no form of life. He brought me to
the time when the earth was void and His Spirit hovered over
the waters. The Lord led me to that very moment when He
said, *"Let us make man in our image."* Right when we were
but a thought in the mind of God.

Like a child, I had so many questions about creation.
Specifically, when Scripture says that God breathed the
"breath of life" into Adam, and He became a living soul.
God created Adam out of the dust, but he wasn't alive until
God breathed on him.

This truth inspired me to dive deeper into the breath of

life. Next, the Lord led me to Ezekiel 37 when it talks about the vision of the dry bones coming to life after God told Ezekiel to prophesy to the bones and tell them to live and they did.

I had a better understanding of how powerful the Word of God is. Just His spoken Word brought the dead to life. Jesus referred to Himself as the Resurrection right before He raised Lazarus from the dead. He is the giver of life! What an important truth to remember.

Between God breathing His very breath into us, depositing His Holy Spirit into us, and Jesus (the living Word) commanding nothing to turn into something, we can see the Holy Trinity at work from the very beginning! I was intrigued by the breath of God and how it causes me to inhale and exhale from my lungs. From that moment on, I never took one breath for granted.

I continued to study on this topic as if God were preparing me for something. I searched the Scriptures and took notes on everything related to the breath of God. I noticed something strange happening.

It was as if the Word of God was speaking to me from the pages. The Scriptures came alive, and it beckoned me to dive deeper in His Word. It was in a way I hadn't done before.

One week, as I prepared to minister in worship, I discovered I would be leading a song that was dear to me. The name of the song is "Great are You Lord." It was a song from Anthony Evans' CD "Altared." I had learned from reading Anthony Evans' track list that this song was listed as "Wynter's Song".

I didn't know who she was, so I looked her up. I immediately balled in tears after learning that she was Anthony's cousin who had died suddenly and unexpectedly at an incredibly young age. What was even more disturbing was learning she and I were the same age at the time of her passing. Life took new meaning after that.

On top of that, Wynter had left behind a husband and four beautiful young girls. I was devastated by this tragedy. I didn't know why I felt so drawn to this family. It was as if the Lord was holding a spotlight on the Evans' family to be a source of strength and encouragement to me.

It wasn't until later that I found out one of her daughters played in one of my favorite movies, "War Room," and she was Priscilla Shirer's cousin. All the people who inspired me were related to each other.

As the Lord began to pour into me about the breath of God and prepared me to minister the song, "Great are you Lord" I was in awe as I sang the part that says, "It's your breath in our lungs, so we pour out our praise." I immediately thought about the moment that Wynter went to bed to take a nap and the Lord took away her breath so she could be with Him in heaven.

The Lord had given and taken back His child. I thought about how peaceful that moment must've been for Wynter. She closed her eyes for a nap and opened them in glory. My heart broke for her family. I'm sure there were many unanswered questions. Some were probably angry, confused, and distraught over losing their loved one unexpectedly. It is very understandable. I'm sure I would be too, but God revealed His sovereignty to me in this season. He taught me that Wynter and every child of God belong to Him first before they belong to anyone else. He also made it clear to me that it is His prerogative who He takes and when.

The Sunday I was due to minister "Wynter's Song", I felt led to share a word the Lord had placed heavily on my heart before singing. This time, I wasn't so sure if what the Lord gave me to share would be received. I had to put my feelings aside and be obedient to Him. That Sunday morning, I felt something leap in my belly. I wasn't pregnant in the natural, but I felt the urge to birth the spiritual baby I know God had placed in me.

Prior to that Sunday, I had given our worship leader a

head's up that I had something the Lord gave me to share. I felt it was important to communicate that out of respect so there would be no surprises. I got the green light and then shared what the Lord gave me.

Before I sang "Great Are You Lord," I gave the congregants a brief synopsis of the song, its meaning and why it was so dear to me. I mentioned Wynter Pitts and that it was her favorite song. I also added that she was a sister in the Lord who had passed away unexpectedly. I didn't know her personally, but she was a believer. So therefore, she IS my sister in Christ. It was strange. Something in me felt that I was not only singing this song as a tribute to the Lord, but also for Wynter.

Anyway, I continued as the Holy Spirit took over and had me testify on the *ruah*, which is Hebrew for the breath of God. At this point, my mind and spirit were two separate entities. My spirit had abandoned me. The Lord took over as I ministered. I felt Him all over me. I realized I had taken quite some time, so I quickly acknowledged the pastor and joked that I wasn't going to preach. I did tell him I needed to birth this baby!

After service, I snuck out the back door and used the backstage exit. Normally after service, I would stay and fellowship with the congregants while refreshments were served in the lobby. My flesh kicked in because I wasn't sure if everyone received the word God gave me. The congregation was about seventy percent Caucasian and Hispanic alike. So, this little black girl had some doubts.

As I headed toward my car, I was stopped by four different congregants who told me how blessed they were by what I shared. One lady even told me she was just studying the *ruah* breath of God the other day! I hugged her in relief and thanked the Holy Spirit for His faithfulness.

Even in my insecurities and doubts, He was right there to reaffirm that this Word needed to be shared. That was one of the many confirmations I had received that week.

The following week after rehearsal, the leadership asked to have a word with me. I sat in anticipation, and I felt the Holy Spirit bracing me for impact. I was told that women were not allowed to teach during worship or preach in front of the congregation where men were present.

I humbly listened as I felt my blood boiling from within. I was completely shocked. This church has a large following and very diverse. I would have never dreamed they would restrict women.

CHAPTER 25

❧

Shake the Dust off Your Feet

"And if any place will not welcome you or listen to you, leave
that place and shake the dust off your feet
as a testimony against them."

(Mark 6:11, NIV)

Most of the churches I had gone to always had male and female evangelists and pastors. Women were never restricted. My former pastors believed that they could not keep a woman from speaking or preaching if she felt conviction from the Lord to do so.

I explained my spiritual background and how I had never heard this until now. I was so disappointed, but more than anything, I was furious. My heart felt as if it was about to explode.

As I tried to listen calmly and attentively, my mind raced to the conversation I knew God and I would have after. I pushed back the tears as soon as they escaped my tear ducts.

I composed myself as best I could and explained that I wasn't trying to defy the rules intentionally. I simply did not know. I also expressed my shock that this was not allowed.

I apologized for appearing to be defiant. But I also made it clear I could not apologize for doing what I know the Lord told me to do. The conversation ended. I stood up, said good night and headed to my car.

As I drove off, I could feel the Lord's presence with me. It was as if He was sitting in the passenger's seat next to me. I felt His silence just waiting for me to break mine, but I couldn't. The tears attempted to escape again, but I just wouldn't give them the satisfaction. I didn't want my core to feel defeated.

My mind wrestled. My thoughts went from pure rage to anger to hurt. How could I be reprimanded for something I was certain God told me to do? I felt as though I had just left the principal's office. My lips still could not find the strength to allow words to be released from them. I felt numb and blindsided. Finally, my voice returned to me as I shouted, "What the heck was that?"

I believe the Holy Spirit was pleased that I had finally released my shock and pain. But then I went numb again. I couldn't believe this was happening to me. Here I was getting another dose of "church hurt." I thought that my days of going into the house of God and leaving worse than I came were over.

But this one was different. It felt different. It wasn't people being human or succumbing to their flesh in anger from a disagreement in ministry. This one was strategic. It was planned. This kind was masked as calm, cool, and collected. It disguised itself as being loving and supportive while attempting to tear and shut me down. This one felt like an all-out spiritual attack. It was the perfect storm.

I finally reached home after circling my block a few times to process my thoughts. I replayed every word trying to make sense of it. I even went back to Sunday when I released what God told me to speak. I never once noticed or observed any sense of disappointment from the leadership. I was puzzled.

When I got inside, I fell to my face. I finally opened the floodgate of tears that had been attempting to come out for the past hour. I found no words. I just sobbed at the feet of the Master. I knew He had heard every utterance and moan. I just let Him hold me. I knew I had been attacked because the Fatherly side of the Holy Spirit was there. He just sat there as I rested my head in His lap. He waited patiently for me to release all the pain and anger I felt. He waited until I was ready to listen.

On Monday, while driving to work, the Lord startled me

with His words. He asked, "What are you doing? I did not create you to be silent. You were attacked precisely because of what I told you to do!" The Lord's voice sounded like thunder in that moment. I cried out, "Lord, what do I do?"

That afternoon, I knew what I had to do. The Lord instructed me to go to the head, the pastor. I was told to hear from the horse's mouth what the church's views were on women in the church. I was also led to speak to him about how intentional God and Jesus were when certain women were either chosen, selected, or validated in Scripture.

One day after service, I made an appointment to speak with the pastor and shared my concerns. He listened patiently and fortified what had been said to me. I spoke my peace and let it be known that as much as I wholeheartedly believe in submission, restricting people because of their gender is wrong and not God's will.

I understood that many churches had embraced the Scripture Paul wrote stating that women should be silent in the church. But it is important to understand it was written in a different time where women were treated unfairly. I believe Paul's words were also taken out of context. Of course, women should submit to their husbands, pastors, and leaders. However, God Himself never said they should be restricted from speaking the Word of God. I posed several questions to the pastor that the Lord gave me.

These questions were also God confirming to me why this was a man-made commission and not of God. For one, why did Jesus appear to Mary first after His resurrection and not the other disciples? Even more so, why did Jesus command her to go and tell the others that He had risen? Would that not make her one of the first evangelists of the gospel? Isn't it the core of the gospel to go and proclaim the death, burial, and resurrection of Jesus Christ?

My second question was, why did Jesus speak to the Samaritan woman at the well? Wasn't it uncommon for Jews to speak with Samaritans in that time? You see, Jesus was and is the Master of tearing down the walls of racism, legalism, and sexism.

He did things His way, not the way of the world. Because of the conversation this Samaritan woman had with Jesus, she was credited with spreading the gospel in Samaria. Samaria to this day has one of the largest Christian populations in Africa. Jesus was intentional in everything He did and every encounter He chose to make. So, who are we to dictate how, and who conveys His message? My last and final point was in the Old Testament.

Why did God choose Esther, a Jewish orphan to be queen? Most importantly, why would He choose her to call three days of fasting and prayer for her people when they were in danger of being annihilated?

She was the one God called to break the traditions and rules of a government system that said the queen could not approach the king unsummoned. To do so meant death. But God granted her favor, and she was able to influence the king. Only the Spirit of God could have given such influence. Ultimately, it was enough to save her people.

Next, what about Deborah? The Lord appointed her as a prophet who would rule and judge her people. She also gave a powerful prophetic word from the Lord that a woman would bring victory to her people. (Judges 4:1-9, 4:17-22) God used a woman, Jael to kill their leader, Sisera instead of Barak, who was the commander of the army. Wasn't God intentional about how those events would be carried out?

I was astonished as the Lord gave me these many occasions in Scripture where *He chose* and decided to use women to bring glory to His name. And let's not forget Mary, the mother of Jesus. God chose a virgin to birth the King of kings. God could have let Jesus simply show up on the scene, be baptized, and fulfill His purpose. But no, God has, is, and will always be intentional about how He chooses to get things done.

Man may have plans, but the steps of the righteous are

ordered by the Lord. I sat and conveyed this message to the pastor. Specifically, in Joel 2:28 when the Lord says, "In the last days, I will pour out my Spirit upon all flesh. Old men will dream dreams and men and my maidens will see visions and prophesy." I left it at that. I didn't argue my case and we agreed to disagree civilly. I did ask the Lord what was the purpose of all of this? He answered, "They won't listen."

I scoffed and responded, "Lord, then why would you have me do this? He reminded me of Moses and how He commanded Moses to confront Pharaoh to let His people go. He reminded me how Pharaoh's heart was hardened even though God commanded Moses to approach him more than once.

Eventually, Pharaoh did let God's people go. But it was not without great suffering, as well as obedience, faith, and trust in God. God performed many miracles in that season. He is the same God I serve today. So that was my stance and my position.

I did what the Lord commanded me. No matter what, I will trust, obey, and see God get the glory even if I don't understand it all. I know in His perfect timing, it will all be revealed. He will fight my battles if I just be still in Him.

We cannot put God in a box and limit what and who God can use. The Lord was teaching me so many valuable lessons here. He taught me that even though He commands me to do something, everyone will not always receive it or agree with it. Beyond that, the Lord taught me that my obedience and submission to Him were of great importance and the most profound lesson.

"Does the Lord delight in burnt offerings and sacrifices as much as in obeying the Lord? To obey is better than sacrifice, and to heed is better than the fat of rams."

(1 Samuel 15:22, NIV)

By submitting to my pastors and leaders even when I felt attacked, rejected, or not heard, I was releasing God to move on my behalf. I didn't need to fight with flesh. I learned that I must war in the Spirit. *"Vengeance is mine, says the Lord."* (Romans 12:19)

The following week, I was up to minister again. I composed myself and allowed the Lord to pour into me. This time, I put on a happy face and did what I was expected to do. I submitted, I worshipped, and I sang. I didn't speak anything else on the microphone, and then I exited the stage. I admit that even with everything going on, my mind was a bit distracted as well. I had just remembered that Anthony Evans was in town again at CBG. I told myself that I would make every effort to be there. I needed a distraction and to be lifted in my spirit.

CHAPTER 26

༜

Repositioned

*"This positioning and repositioning by God are so very important,
especially at this season, because God is making sure we are at
the correct battle stations in this final war of all wars! You will
see that all that you have been through has trained you for your
assigned battle station. Nobody else can do your assignment!
Everything that has happened to you in your life was permitted by
God and will work for your good and His glory! Praise Him!"*
(Henry Walker)

As we finished our worship set, I left quickly and called
up Cynthia to see if she wanted to go with me. It was
because of Cynthia that I even became a fan of Anthony
Evans. His CD had been on rotation nonstop since I had first
seen him. One of his famous covers called "Raise a
Hallelujah" was getting me through this ordeal. I decided to
praise instead of complaining. Praise became my weapon
against the Enemy.

A few minutes after rushing home to grab a bite before heading out, Cynthia called me. She said she couldn't make it because she was under the weather. I had been battling a cold as well, but I didn't want to miss this. I felt disappointed that my girl couldn't go. I almost talked myself out of going because I didn't want to go alone.

As soon as my mind tried to get me to stay home, I heard the voice of God say, *"This is your journey to take, not hers."* I was filled with holy fear as the Lord's voice sounded stern. I quickly snapped out of my pity party and headed toward the door. Before leaving, I went on my knees and asked for God's favor and protection. I wasn't sure why I felt a sense of urgency to do so, but I didn't question it. I obeyed.

The drive from my home to CBG was about forty minutes. The ride there was unbelievably peaceful. I worshipped God while listening to Anthony Evans' CD all the way there.

When I came close to the church, I sighed in relief and praise that the Lord got me there safely. I felt anxious and excited as I approached *Church by the Glades*. There was something different in how I felt pulling up to CBG. For the first time, it felt familiar. It felt as if I was coming home.

CBG always overwhelmed me with its huge size. Thanksgiving was approaching, so the holiday season was in full effect. The festive decorations were so beautiful in the lobby. I arrived an hour early because I wanted to get a good seat this time. The last time I was there, my girls and I all decided to go, but we were late. CBG fills up quickly, so I wanted to ensure I got close enough to see and enjoy worship.

The sign outside said the doors would open fifteen minutes prior to service. I sat down near the café and did a little people watching. For some reason, I was praying that God would grant me favor. I didn't understand why I kept praying for favor, but I guess my spirit was praying for me.

I looked at my phone to see the time and it was still early. I heard the voice of the Lord again. He said get up and get in line; don't miss this. I was puzzled at the urgency of the Lord regarding this visit to CBG. I didn't understand it all, but again, I obeyed. I got up and stood next to the entrance door. A line had not formed yet, but as soon as I got up, it did instantaneously! I smiled at the Holy Spirit for His wisdom and thanked Him too.

As I stood waiting, the line got longer. I was so thankful that I wasn't way in the back. I glanced at my phone again and felt butterflies in my stomach. What was happening? Why was I so excited? I mean I was a fan and loved Anthony Evans' music, but this felt strange. It felt divine.

186

A few seconds later, the doors flew open and the Holy Spirit shouted "Go!" People rushed in trying not to run. I smirked and whispered again "God, give me favor." Walking in there felt like a dream.

There was a rush and chaos all around me, but I felt an inner calm over me. I headed to the front row and the seats were all labeled "reserved." So, I went to the second row. I sat relieved that I had gotten a good seat. But something was bothering me.

Now, this may sound vain and arrogant, so I apologize in advance. Remember when I said it was around the holidays? Well, in South Florida, you rarely get the chance to sport your winter gear and boots. Well, your girl here was wearing black knee-high boots with gold buckles and a black leather jacket that matched with gold zipper accents. I don't know why this was so important to me, but all I could think of was "Nobody can see my boots in the second row!" I laughed at myself and sat there waiting for the service to start. It felt more like waiting for a show or performance the way the church was set up. I could never get over the overwhelming feeling of the beautiful stage lights and the details of the stage that CBG did every service. I looked around anticipating just being in the presence of God and worshiping Him.

I decided to browse through my phone to pass time. Suddenly, a middle-aged woman of European descent approached me and asked if I could give up my seat. I looked at her feeling like Rosa Parks.

I attempted to swallow any ounce of rudeness and asked, "Where am I going to sit?" She smiled and explained to me that she had guests in town and wanted everyone to sit together in the row. They were short one seat. My seat would be the one to accommodate her guests. She said, "Let me ask the host if she can find you another seat." I looked around as the woman caught the attention of the host to talk to her while pointing at me. I must admit that I felt strange and wondered what was going on.

I watched the host attentively and wondered if this woman was really about to make me get up. The host nodded at the older woman and signaled for me to come to her. I asked as calmly as possible, "Where am I supposed to sit?" She pointed to a front row seat right in the middle-labeled VIP/Reserved and said, "You can sit right here." I thanked her and sat down with tears in my eyes. I shook my head in awe smiling to God and thanking Him in my seat.

Of course, He was behind this! The Lord repositioned me to a seat in the front row that He had reserved just for me! I praised God silently in my chair and decided that I was not going to act as if I didn't belong in that seat.

I am a child of the King! Of course, I had the right to be in that seat as much as anyone else. I was in tears at the Lord's faithfulness and how He even accommodated the silent desires of my heart to be in the front. He strategically had me sit where I was so that the older woman could ask me for my seat to position me in the front. Wow!

As Anthony Evans came out, I was a bit starstruck. I didn't know whether I should take out my camera phone or just worship. I did both, still amazed at how God had positioned me.

Anthony was standing right in front of me on stage. I was so close that I could see his teeth and every facial movement he made. I praised God and worshipped the Lord that night with so much gratitude! I didn't quite understand why the Lord did it, but I was thankful.

CHAPTER 27

❧

Abba, the Bridegroom,
&
The Coronation

"The bride belongs to the bridegroom.
The friend who attends the bridegroom waits and listens for
him and is full of joy when he hears the bridegroom's voice.
That joy is mine, and it is now complete."
(John 3:29, NIV)

W ithin the next stage of my journey, another shift took place. God planted a spiritual seed in me that was growing. My spirit felt more synthesized and in tune with His voice. The Lord had me dig deeper into His Word regarding the future.

The Lord led me to search Scripture about prophecies and prophets He used in the days of old. I studied Samuel, Ezekiel, Jeremiah, Nathan, Elijah, and Elisha.

I was taken aback at how the Lord had spoken His Word to His servants and the miraculous signs and wonders He performed on their behalf. God the Father was speaking, and I was finally learning how to position myself to hear Him.

Dreams, visions, and passions that I had for my life were being resurrected in my spirit. Ideas and thoughts that I had placed on the back burner of my mind started to take shape. Desires and aspirations that I wanted to achieve became realities in my spirit. God was showing me that those dreams were placed in me by Him. The Enemy had done all he could to delay God's plan for my life, but he failed.

I started to nurture and feed my spiritual baby with the Word of God. I began applying God's Word to my life as the Lord led me. He said His Word is alive, a two-edged sword. I had to learn to speak over my situations and circumstances with the Word of God. I started journaling more and memorizing Scripture. I learned how to combat the Enemy the way Jesus did when He was tempted by the Devil. I declared, "It is written."

In the months that followed, I felt as if I was in preparation mode but what I was being prepared for, I wasn't sure. Soon after, a global pandemic hit the United States and the entire world. A virus called Covid-19 had come to our shores, causing thousands and thousands of deaths.

The virus caused flu-like symptoms and made it difficult

to breathe. Young and old around the world were consumed. Doctors, nurses, and first responders were all declared heroes during this time because they were putting themselves at risk every day to help save people's lives.

Soon after, in March of 2020, my school decided to close because of the virus. Businesses, restaurants, and schools all around the country embraced a massive shut down. People were encouraged to stay at home and to not leave unless necessary. Fear and uncertainty filled the earth.

It was a difficult season to be in. Millions of people had to file for unemployment due to being laid off from their jobs. People panicked and were without food or financial resources. This was a time to either live by faith or succumb to fear. Racial and social injustice also reared its ugly head during this pandemic.

An African American man by the name of George Floyd was killed at the hands of a police officer and people wanted justice. Protests, riots, and looting ensued because black, brown, and white people were tired of this. Too many times, young black men and women had been brutally murdered at the hands of white individuals. Specifically, some who vowed to protect and serve. Through all of this, I asked God a question because I knew somewhere in the midst of all of this chaos, He was going to move in a mighty way.

One night, while sitting and praying to God about this "new normal" we were in, I asked *"God, what are you up to?"* God in His infinite wisdom revealed to me that Covid-19 and this season of social unrest was a time to hit the pause button and seek His face. The Lord provided a portal of time for His children to reset and reprioritize their relationships with Him, their families, and friends. God poured into me so much during the pandemic.

It was a season where I saw many prayers answered. Before Covid-19, I had always prayed for more time to rest and focus on my goals and dreams. I never imagined that it would come in this form filled with such hurt, pain, and tragedy. Yet I have learned that if there is free will, evil always has a door to enter. We just aren't always alerted in which form it will come. Pain, sickness, hate, murder, are all matters we see in this world. But in God's kingdom, His will is always done.

My heart went out to the many lives that were lost. This virus hit home to many families. For me, it is a constant reminder of how precious life is. I learned how to be thankful to God for the many things we tend to take for granted: life, love, family, and the power of community.

Words like purpose and destiny were being echoed into my spirit. Positioning and alignment were the marching orders I heard from the Spirit of God. Worship and praise were more of a necessity as I spent more and more time in the presence of the Lord.

God was speaking, moving, and shifting things for His glory. He was also uncovering and exposing the plans of the Enemy to those whose eyes and ears were inclined to His Spirit. God was raising up an army. He took His rightful place as Commander-in-Chief in my life.

Through pain, anxiety, anger, frustration, and uncertainty, I saw the hand of God moving. The Lord revealed to me that He is my Shepherd. He declared that He spoke over me and that I was not to listen to anyone else who spoke over me without consulting Him first.

The Father revealed Himself to me as Abba, which in Hebrew means "Daddy." His adoption of me as His daughter has changed the trajectory of my identity. I officially became His daughter this season.

I sought, worshipped, and obeyed my King in this season as never before. I experienced and encountered God in an intimate and special way. I related to the Father, and He related to me. I felt the love of the Father through countless miracles, provisions, and acts of kindness from others. He provided every need I had after I lost my main source of income. I received the most precious gift in this season. Abba gave me a glimpse of me in Eden. I was *resurrected, redeemed, and restored.*

My focus and agenda pivoted during this time. I became more intentional about matters pertaining to the kingdom of heaven. I saw more clearly that this earth is not my home. The Lord constantly reminded me to abide in Him as He abides in me. He taught me that if I kept my eyes on Him, everything would work out for His glory and my good.

The Lord often refers to Himself as a farmer in Scripture. He frequently told parables about seeds, sowing, and reaping as references to the kingdom. The more I thought of it, the more I realized I was a seed.

Not only me, but all of God's children are seeds He has planted in His garden. The Lord planted and replanted me until I was in fertile ground.

He fertilized me with gifts and abilities to reach the world for His kingdom. The Lord invested in me. He pruned and plucked the weeds of the Enemy from around me. He gave me the Son to grow and develop me. He gave me water when I was in a dry desert, thirsty for Him.

God is the Great Farmer and a good Father. My Father has uncovered and healed me of hidden hurts and pains I held on to for years. He has placed His Spirit in me. That Spirit has birthed boldness and an awakening of His presence in my life. He has restored me as a child of God. He has drawn me closer in a spiritually intimate way. He has adopted me as His daughter.

The Lord continues to discipline and correct me when I'm wrong or miss the mark. Conviction will fall upon me whenever I am filled with pride, fear, and doubt. But I am grateful even for that. It means His Spirit is near. "The Lord corrects the people He loves and disciplines those He calls His own." (Hebrews 12:6)

God has awarded me with His promises of yes and amen. I am still on this journey, but I am glad my true identity has been defined by the King. I have become God's daughter.

The Lord has been faithful to me and to all of creation. In the beginning, His ultimate purpose of creating man and woman was for us to have an intimate relationship with Him. The signs of the times are already here. The earth has already begun to produce the birthing pains of what is to come.

Pandemics, racism, sexism, injustice, wars, and famine are our reality. The kingdom of God is near. God is calling His sons and daughters to the front lines. He is depending on us to bear fruit for Him. The Father took a great risk by sending His Son Jesus to die for all of us. He knew some would receive the Truth, and some would deny it.

Our heavenly Father risked it all for you and me. God planted you into His beautiful garden. One day soon, Jesus will crack the sky and come for His bride—a bride without a spot or wrinkle. I encourage you as a daughter or son of God to allow Him to prune and prepare you. Allow the Father to mold and shape you as His own. The earth is waiting with expectation for the children of God to be revealed. *"The whole creation waits breathless with anticipation for the revelation of God's sons and daughters."* (Romans 8:19)

I pray that on that day, you will be counted as a daughter or son of God. In the meantime, I will continue to run this race and allow His light to shine in and through me. I will continue to deny my flesh, so that His Holy Spirit may live through me. I pray that when the Father comes to reap His harvest, you and I will be as beautiful sunflowers with many seeds attached to them.

I never imagined that my life would've taken the many twists and turns that it did. I always knew that my Creator had a plan for me. But I never imagined that He would call me to be a part of His family. I have learned to trust and depend on the giver of life. I have learned to be obedient and bold for the glory of His kingdom. The Lord has taught me how to surrender my weaknesses and failures at His feet. He is a good, good Father. He has taken my guilt, shame, and brokenness. He has exchanged my burdens for the blessing of Abraham. I wait for that great day to see Him face-to-face.

In Revelation 21, we see the newness of life being established. *(Please see Revelation 21:1-27)*. On that day, there will be a new heaven, a new earth and a new bride. The bride is me. The bride is you, if you so choose. The wedding date has been set by the Father. Jesus has provided a place for me.

He did not hesitate to put a ring on it. He wants to do the same for you too! Say yes to Him for eternity. Just say yes!

A glimpse into our wedding day...
Revelation 21:1-3; 21:6-7; 9-10

"Then I saw a new heaven and a new earth for the first heaven and the first earth had passed away, and there was no longer any sea. I saw the Holy City, the New Jerusalem, coming down out of heaven from God, prepared as a bride beautifully dressed for her husband. And I heard a loud voice from the throne saying, "Look! God's dwelling place is now among the people, and he will dwell with them. They will be his people, and God himself will be with them and be their God."

"He said to me: 'It is done. I am the Alpha and the Omega, the Beginning and the End. To the thirsty I will give water without cost from the spring of the water of life. Those who are victorious will inherit all this, and I will be their God and they will be my children.'"

"One of the seven angels who had the seven bowls full of the seven last plagues came and said to me, "Come, I will show you the bride, the wife of the Lamb." And he carried me away in the Spirit to a mountain great and high, and showed me the Holy City, Jerusalem, coming down out of heaven from God."

Our Wedding, The Coronation...

There I am. Walking toward the throne of God. The Lion and the Lamb, my Bridegroom is at the right hand of the Father. He waits for me as I glide toward Him with love, joy, and affection in my eyes. I am clothed in all white. My head is adorned with a golden crown. He watches me with fire in His eyes. I must look away because the radiance and light surrounding Him blinds me.

He is beautiful to behold. I walk thinking, *how did I become so fortunate? Why did He choose me? I am not worthy of His love.* As I approach the throne, I kneel and lay my crown at His feet. He takes my hand and I glance at His nail-pierced wrists. He then presents me to His Father, *our Father*.

I am overwhelmed and filled with ecstasy. I am ransomed and redeemed. I have been accepted and perfected in His sight. My new body is built for eternity. We walk side by side and I glance at His face. There is no need for the sun anymore. The Son lights up the new heaven. I look down and the streets are paved with gold. His smile melts my soul. We have become one.

My Bridegroom will be crowned the King of kings and Lord of lords. I can't wait to see my Master, Savior, and Creator face-to-face. The blood of Jesus has given me the opportunity to be called His bride. I am not worthy but through His sacrifice, He calls me His own.

The courageous Lion who appeared in my dream sacrificed His life and fought to save me. I saw love and devotion in His eyes. The Lion of Judah became the sacrificial Lamb for the world He created.

Accepting the gift of salvation through Jesus Christ was more than just becoming a Christian. It was a calling into a deeper relationship with the Father through His Son, Jesus. It is a daily process of becoming less of me and you. It is to deny yourself for Him. When I accepted Jesus, I became the bride of Christ and a joint heir in the kingdom of heaven. Most importantly, I became who I was created to be…

-A Daughter of God.

"God was kind and decided that Christ would choose us to be God's own adopted children."
(Ephesians 1:5)

"All of you are God's children because of your faith in Christ Jesus."
(Galatians 3:26)

"Bride of the King, listen carefully to me. Forget your own people and your father's family. The King adores you. He is your Master, so do what he desires."
(Psalm 45:10)

"Fear not, Daughter of Zion; behold, your King is coming."
(John 12:15, ESV)

The Farmer will Return...

ACKNOWLEDGEMENTS
❧

I would like to thank my parents, family and friends for your constant support throughout my life. Your faith, prayers and encouragement mean the world to me, and I am forever grateful. I love you all to life and there's nothing you can do about it!

To my publisher, Karolyne Roberts and the entire **Luminous Publishing** Team; Thank you for taking a chance with me and being obedient to the Holy Spirit of God. Your knowledge, guidance, humility and grace taught me a lot during the editing process, and I am so glad to have gained a sister in Christ while birthing this baby of mine! The best is yet to come Sis!

To my spiritual covering, Pastor Toure' Roberts; Thank you and **The Potter's House One LA** team for your constant prayers, support and leadership during the pandemic and beyond!

To Pastor David and Lisa Hughes and the **Church by the Glades** family; Thank you for your constant support and for creating an atmosphere where Jesus Christ is a Superstar, the gospel is preached, and the church body feels like home.